Praise for *Go with the Flow Stress & Pain Release Guide*

"Ingenious! A simple, free, self-help method to reduce stress and get out of pain. It doesn't get any better than that."
—Dr. Matthew Shepherd - Chiropractor

"*Go with the Flow Stress & Pain Release Guide* has many immediate, useful tools to help anyone with stress and pain. Gina shares many insights that help us navigate the path of life with more joy and effectiveness."
—Benjamin Ling, M.D.

"A 'medical intuitive,' Gina Giacomini uses her personal journey of discovery, curiosity and experience to understand the roots of physical distress. In plain language, she describes the conditions that foster, sustain and alleviate pain and stress. *Go with the Flow Stress & Pain Release Guide* is a well-articulated book that integrates multiple perspectives of healing."
—Stephen Curtin, Ph.D. - Clinical Psychologist

"*Go with the Flow Stress & Pain Release Guide* has a down-to-earth approach to deal with life's stress and pain. Gina's quick, simple techniques fit easily into a busy day."
—William R. Wills, R.Ph., GE - Compounding Pharmacist

Go with the Flow

STRESS & PAIN RELEASE GUIDE

Go with the Flow

STRESS & PAIN RELEASE GUIDE

Easy-to-Use Tools to Energize Your Life

Gina Giacomini

INNERVISIONS
PUBLICATIONS

Coloma, CA

Published by: **Innervisions Publications**
   P. O. Box 213
   Coloma, CA 95613

Editors: Roberta Wedan, Tom Fisher, Diana Sherer
Book Design: Jerry Ashburn
Formatting: James Marquez
www.earthtrekexpeditions.com
Illustrations: Rick Meadows
Photographs: Stephanie Gabler
www.gablerfamilyphotography.com
Model: Elizabeth Gabler

Printed in the United States of America

  Publisher's Cataloging-in-Publication Data
Giacomini, Gina.
 Go with the flow stress & pain release guide : easy-to-use tools to energize your life / Gina Giacomini.
  p. cm.
 ISBN: 978-0-96694-271-2
 1. Pain—therapy. 2. Stress management. 3. Mind and body. I. Title.
 RB127 .G52 2010
 612.8—dc22

          2010927674

With special thanks to:

Ellen, once again you provided the expertise, support and enthusiasm that helped me complete the book

Roberta, for your wonderful friendship, editing expertise and mathematical mind

Jerry, for your creative and artistic talent, patience and generosity

James, your patience, expertise and direction were instrumental throughout this book

Steph, my great friend, business manager, photographer and motivator

Tink, a wonderful and very patient model

Tom, your uncanny ability to see what didn't work and ask, "What does this mean?"

Tyler, for your Indesign expertise, patience and love

Courtney, Cole & Mason, for your love and support

Maureen, without your help and support, I wouldn't be writing today

Gia, for your internet wizardry and insight

Grandpa & Dan, for your kindness, generosity and all around fun

Matt, for the needed attitude adjustments and support

Ben, for the gift of your direction, kindness and friendship

Dr. Kal, for your belief in me, friendship and stimulating conversations

Erin, my dear friend who kept me stress-free with her great massages

Steve, for your encouragement, friendship and wood for the winter

My clients, for allowing me to be part of their healing process

The Ganga river group, who shared their fun and enthusiasm with me

This book is dedicated to Steve Armantrout aka Stevie Wonder, my best friend and fellow river guide for twenty years. A light has gone out in the world with your passing. However, your spirit and shining example of adventure, music, laughter and loving life continues...

A special dedication to Raven, Zeke and Sweet Tree, who taught me unconditional love the only way pets can, and to enjoy the little things life has to offer.

Contents

Introduction

Unconsciousness, spontaneity, instinct...hold us to the earth and dictate the relatively good and useful.
—**Henri Frederic Amiel**

We live in an age of immediate information, instant gratification and constant transition. Trying to keep up with advances in science, the economy and world affairs all too often leaves us exhausted and disillusioned. Most of us respond by moving at a quicker pace, multi-tasking throughout our day, setting our sights on the end of the day when we finally relax. Unfortunately, this harried pace pushes us out of the moment and into overdrive. We may accomplish all our tasks, although it's usually at the expense of enjoying the day. By evening there isn't much energy left for what is most important—ourselves and our family. With the outer world in chaos, we are stretched beyond our limits. **Now is the time to look within for peace, release and answers.**

This book is designed to release stress and pain using a whole body approach. Throughout your body, you have inner instincts and senses waiting to be activated. Stress and pain tend to force the body into a "fight or flight" response while interrupting the communication between your body, emotions and mind. **Rediscover your instinctual self and insight—and re-humanize your life.** The simple step-by-step techniques in this book allow you to respond to stress and pain using an inner approach. It is essentially a comprehensive manual of techniques that I've discovered and developed during twenty years of teaching intuition and stress release skills. All of these techniques are based on simple principles. Some of the information was graciously taught to me by teachers and mentors. Other parts came as flashes of inspiration or were discovered while working with people's energy, the rest were forged through personal adversity.

Chapter 1 gives you an understanding of how stress and pain affect the body. Chapter 2 provides the overall philosophy of the book—utilizing strength along with your will to accomplish tasks. Chapter 3 shows the benefits of changing from a mental focus to a whole body awareness. Chapter 4 engages your inner core and calm center. Chapter 5 instructs how to set goals or intentions from within for quick results. Chapter 6 helps you more fully utilize two energy sources for your physical body. Chapter 7 provides ways to give your body a secure base instead of operating in survival mode. Chapter 8 allows you to create healthy boundaries with built-in reaction time. Chapter 9 gives you a road map of your body. Chapter 10 explains personal space with built-in reaction time. Chapter 11 shows ways to utilize your intuition throughout the day. Chapter 12 offers insight into your primary and secondary functions and how they impact your life. Chapter 13 integrates all of the "daily survival skills" into one easy package.

Each chapter discusses an important principle and provides personal experiences, client anecdotes and easy techniques to practice throughout the book. Each technique builds on the previous one and can be completed in a matter of moments when time is short, or enjoyed more fully when time allows. Use these tools at the start of your day or during lulls in your daily activities—such as waiting for your computer to boot up, standing in line at a store or on hold during a phone call. Take a few moments to try these techniques to improve your focus and realign your psyche without disrupting normal routines.

Some people willingly look inside for a different approach. Others are forced by stressful circumstances to look within for answers. In either instance, it is important to acknowledge that a decision to look within ultimately leads to a deeper connection with the undiscovered self. Since some of these parts reside in the subconscious, they have their own agendas—which don't align with your conscious goals. These parts hinder your progress and keep you unfocused. When you tap into your instincts and insight, your sub-conscious and conscious parts come together and you immediately feel more whole. Using both your five outer senses and the corre-sponding inner senses together heightens and expands your awareness.

An important point to remember when starting the process is this: anything you try on an inner level is accomplished by allowing, rather than pushing or controlling. Allowing life to flow through you at first may feel unusual. However, trying to control anything is an illusion since life is uncertain and always changing.

Slow down, find your rhythm and establish a reasonable pace at the start of a busy day. With this approach, you intuitively know when to move forward, when to pause and reflect, and most impor-tantly, when to stop working and rest. The payoff is less stress and pain, recognition of more opportunities and the ability to realize your potential.

Release stress and pain

with...

A whole body approach

to life

Chapter 1

What is Stress?

Stress is when your gut says, "No way,"
and your mouth says, "Sure, no problem."
—RRP

In today's fast-paced world, one thing most of us have in common is stress. The dictionary defines stress as "pressure that is affecting something or someone due to an external force." When we lead a healthy and balanced life, stress is a positive catalyst that engages and refines our instincts. We react to stress using a whole body approach involving our body, emotions and intellect. For example, if the physical body is threatened or in distress, it reacts instinctively with a "fight or flight" response. Our emotions, the bridge between the body and intellect, react to this signal and send out a warning. In turn, the mind responds with a solution. All of this happens so quickly that most of the time we are unaware this communication transpires.

Unfortunately, chronic stress for a prolonged period of time has a negative effect. It adversely affects our instincts, sending them into a survival response. In turn, this interrupts communication between the mind, body and emotions, cutting off the natural energy flow. As demands and deadlines increase, multitasking and compartmentalizing become the daily routine, while we try our best to keep up the pace. As we continue to push our physical body beyond its limits, we deplete its energy supply. When our body runs low on energy, we often turn to artificial stimuli for help—caffeine, nicotine, drugs, alcohol or adrenaline. These methods are a temporary fix. Although we keep up the pace, we end up with less energy and more stress.

15

As a result, we walk around unaware that our physical body is in a constant state of survival.

Rediscover your instincts and intuition with a whole body approach to life. Communication is then restored between the body, mind and emotions, and you experience your natural state of being.

What is Pain?

Your pain is the breaking of the shell
that encloses your understanding.
—Kahlil Gibran

The dictionary defines pain as "the sensation that is felt when you are hurt physically, emotionally or mentally." When a portion of the body is in pain or distress, most of us react by ignoring it, masking it with medication, focusing on it too much or isolating it with sheer will. These solutions are understandable responses to meet the demands of life. Most of the time these approaches work. Since the pain cycle is interrupted, the body can relax and its natural energy flow is restored. This allows the pain to leave. However, in chronic pain situations, these same solutions trap pain within the body and cut off the natural energy flow. When this occurs, it creates more issues in the long run than the original problem.

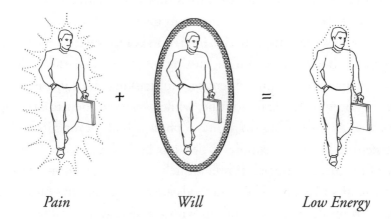

| Pain | Will | Low Energy |

Remember—pain is a signal warning you some part of your psyche is in distress and needs attention. The old saying "Don't shoot the messenger" is valid when it relates to pain. Instead, why not try a different approach? When pain strikes, remember it is a warning to slow down—some part of you is signaling that something is wrong. If you ignore the signs and keep forcing your body with will, it won't cooperate. Since your physical body is not cognitive, you can't reason with it. When pushed too far, it resists any will-driven push to get well by shutting down and holding on.

This book provides easy-to-use techniques to reduce stress and pain, engage your instincts, set healthy boundaries, increase your intuition and enhance your life at work and home.

Learn:

Focus: Shift from a mental focus to a whole body awareness. This gives your mind a break and allows your body to return to its natural state of balance.

Grounding: Give your physical body a secure base and it rewards you by letting go of stress and pain. When your body feels safe and out of survival mode, stress and pain automatically release.

Boundaries: Create healthy boundaries with built-in reaction time. These techniques work well in person and on the phone.

Energy: Release physical, emotional or mental distress the quickest way possible—energetically.

(These skills will re-humanize your life)

The underlying philosophy

of this book

is...

Understanding

strength and will

Chapter 2

Strength and Will

But the tides are always shifting
The land is never still.
You can not tame a river
And bend it to your will.
                    —**Betsy Rose**

As we go through life, we are taught two separate sets of skills. The world teaches us to take action, control our thoughts, manage our time and maintain self-control. We learn from an early age to enlist our mind and *will* to deal with these demands of the world.

By contrast, nature teaches us different skills—to let go, allow, take things in stride and adapt, since circumstances are always changing. Life's flow can be summed up in the word *strength*. It is accessed through the heart.

Will is like a train speeding down a track; its main purpose is its destination. If there are obstacles in the way, a train mows down whatever is on the tracks. Similarly, when our main focus is meeting deadlines, we are on a fast track and attempting to control life. Pushing our way through the day's agenda alienates people around us, causing us to miss significant opportunities. We ignore the day's rhythms and cycles which help us accomplish what is most important. Ironically, in trying to control life, we limit it.

Strength, on the other hand, is like a flowing river. It winds its way around obstacles, making them smooth with its constant motion. There are parts of the river that are extremely rough and dangerous. Luckily, there are also long stretches of calm water.

19

Whether the water is rough or calm, the flow of the river, like the flow of life, is always there spurring us on. **Start the day connecting with the flow, and the day's journey becomes as important as the destination.**

Will is an important part of the psyche that is necessary for survival. However, our will becomes problematic when relied on exclusively. When life feels scary and out of control, we resort to our mind and will to cope, ignoring the physical and emotional responses. This results in neglecting our physical and emotional needs. Living life exclusively through will causes tension, stress, pain and disease.

Imagine your will as a mighty oak tree. Oak is a very strong wood, but it is not at all flexible. In heavy winds, oak trees break. Strength is like a supple reed, whose greatest asset is its flexibility. The reed bends when the workload is overwhelming. **Use strength along with will each day and balance both sides of your nature. You'll recognize when your load is too heavy and make the adjustments needed.**

An excellent way to start your day is taking a few moments to connect with strength and plug into life's flow. You'll feel more adaptable and flexible instead of pushing your way through the day to complete everything on your agenda. When you push too hard, it creates resistance and missed opportunities, significantly slowing your productivity.

When you find yourself feeling stressed and inflexible, take a few moments to balance your will with strength. Taking a short break may seem difficult on a busy day, but reconnecting with life's flow positively affects an entire day's outcome. Don't be surprised when you bump into the person you've been trying to reach or find the solution to the problem you need to solve. Events like these happen when you relax and are present enough to recognize the opportunities. See circumstances change on an outer level by connecting with life's flow on an inner level.

A significant aspect of strength is trusting in adversity. At times life is difficult and unmanageable. It can seem too much for one person to handle. However, by shifting your focus to strength when chaos strikes, you'll find life's flow working in the midst of it. Meeting life's challenges is like paddling into white-water rapids—stay present, pay attention, rely on your instincts and hang on. Whether or not you stay in the boat, strength provides the trust needed to handle the experience. Don't misunderstand me, your will should not go away. That driving force within you is necessary to meet life's challenges. However, connecting with life's flow and strength along with your will creates a better balance.

Personally, I found this to be true soon after I divorced. I made the decision to live through strength, and trust that life would provide what I needed. This meant making a conscious effort to align with life's flow. It seemed like a good choice at the time, since I didn't have much to lose. That summer, I rented a small cabin on the American River and became a river guide. In retrospect, I see that life gave me a front row seat to study a perfect symbol of strength—the river.

Since then, the river seems to mirror my life. During my first summer as a guide, I learned to look ahead to see where I wanted to position my boat. In my life as well, I had to look ahead to see which direction to take. I had a strong desire to work with children, and that fall, I found a job teaching in a home-study program.

Each year, I learn new lessons from the river. One year was a low water season with rocks in the river I had never noticed before. Similarly, in my personal life and at work, it seemed all I dealt with were obstacles. Another year, I was attempting to hold down three jobs to make ends meet—I was on the verge of falling apart physically, mentally and emotionally. At the point of desperation, I made an important if not obvious realization: If I continued to cope using only my will, I wouldn't survive much longer. I decided to reduce my workload and slow down to keep my sanity. Before I knew it, I was laid off from one job. It seemed the decision to change my workload was out of my control, just like experiencing a class V rapid. Later on, I realized this situation helped me trust in adversity. As it turned out, I survived financially and managed to be a sane mother. Being receptive and accepting of this situation allowed me to recognize that life's flow was with me. One less job helped me slow down. I was able to stay in the moment and use my creativity to make ends meet instead of pushing myself with only my will.

Two years later, a flood washed away my riverfront cabin. Luckily, I had moved the previous year and was living in a home 150 feet from the river's edge. That year, I was glad to be part of life's flow, rather than in the way of the river's flow.

From an entrepreneur: "I've never had a typical profession, schedule or paycheck. I make my living in a variety of ways. This includes mining, construction, cutting firewood and stock trading. I count on intuition and life's flow to bring me what I need. Before the start of mining season, I make sure to sell several ounces of gold. On some level it leaves a space and signals life to provide me what I need."

This book teaches you allowing techniques based on strength and insight. Together, these skills lead to a path of healing and wholeness.

Intuition is the ability to access insight and understanding without conscious reasoning. Although your outer senses guide you in every day life, you also use inner senses and instincts. Intuition delivers this information quickly and efficiently in the form of hunches, gut feelings, sensing, pictures, flashes of insight and inner knowing.

Small children instinctively rely on their intuition and life's flow. As they grow, they are taught to depend more on outer senses. As they become adults, the insights are not strongly felt or are often ignored.

What stops most people from actively accessing their intuition? The biggest hindrance is stress and pain. People in distress use only a fraction of their mental and emotional abilities and a small portion of insight and instincts. Pain and stress also affect the ability of the outer and inner senses to work together, causing responses predominantly through mental or emotional functions. A mental approach often leads to immediate solutions. Unfortunately, frustration sets in later, since emotions weren't involved in the decision-making. Likewise, an emotional response elicits a solution that seems to work. Hindsight reveals the consequences of not seeing the bigger picture. Intuition bridges the gap between logic and emotions, going beyond what the outer senses are capable of perceiving.

When I first started teaching intuition courses, I wasn't convinced I was ready to take on what seemed such a daunting task. However, I was convinced that whatever skills I shared should be useful, practical and ethical. I spent time examining the steps needed to consciously access the inner senses and guidance. **My first question involved the difference between giving information based on opinion as opposed to information involving insight.** I noticed when I offered my opinion, it was a combination of thought processes or emotional reactions to the situation. Equally involved were my ego, my limited belief system and "how the day was going." However, when I offered information based on insight, it was free of these influences and came from a different place. **After much trial and error, I realized the best place to access my insight was through my heart, the pathway to my instincts, inner senses and personal truth.** Unlike other methods, my heart did not manipulate my intuition. Meeting my insight with an open heart, it did not mislead me.

The next step called for a huge leap of trust. I learned to express the first feeling, thought, sense or picture that came to me and say it out loud. Once I spoke the words aloud, the flow of information took a form of its own. I also noticed the words I spoke had a different resonance and power behind them. This realization is a most important discovery when accessing intuition. **When you say a word out loud from your heart, the intention behind the word resonates and manifests quickly in the physical world.**

Over the last twenty years, I simplified and refined this concept, choosing key words that use specific intentions and are designed to release stress and pain, balance the body and offer direct access to your intuition. You will find key words throughout this book.

Key Word #1 *Strength*: The intention behind the key word, "**Strength**," is connecting to life's flow. In doing so, you balance your will with strength and stay present in the moment.

Key Word #2 *Center*: The key word, "**Center**," is a signal for you to let go of control and focus on your heart center. Since your mind is not in charge, sit back, relax and experience what happens next.

Key Word #3 *Core*: Access your inner core, which houses your inner instincts and insight, by saying, "**Core**," out loud from your heart.

Life constantly challenges us to experience what children do naturally; slow down, find our own pace and work within life's balance. In allowing strength to become an important part of the day, you align with the flow, accomplish what is most important and still enjoy the day.

A former insurance risk manager's anecdote: "My wife started Gina's course. After a few weeks, I noticed a transformation in her. I decided to share in these changes so I started the course a few months later. In the first classes, we learned about the different aspects of strength and will; the journey being as important as the destination. I worked as a risk manager at the time, and every Monday morning, I started work with a severe headache. The class helped me realize that I used my will to cope with my stressful job. After I worked with my will part, the headaches disappeared. Soon after, I decided to change my career and be more pro-active instead of reactive in my life. I now work in education."

Strength and Will Technique

Key Word: "Strength"
Allow this technique to happen rather than forcing it.
Sit back, relax and experience the flow.

~Take a few moments in the morning to connect with life's flow; at home, at work or in your car.

~Sit in a quiet place and close your eyes. Shift your focus from head to heart by placing your hand on the middle of your chest. Take a few moments to focus there.

~Press in firmly at your chest, take a deep breath and imagine you are breathing in life's flow. Hold the breath for five seconds. As you breathe out, release any excess will or control.

~Next, place your hands on your lap, palms toward the ceiling. Say the key word, **"Strength,"** out loud from your heart. Feel a calm energy enter your hands, flow up your arms, into your neck and head, down your back and out your legs and feet.

~Sink into this energy for a minute or two. You are now part of life's flow and are an integral part of the universe.

Quick Version: Place one hand on the middle of your chest and focus there. Take a deep breath, hold for five seconds and as you breathe out, release any excess will or control. Place your hands on your lap, palms toward the ceiling and say the key word, **"Strength,"** out loud from your heart. Allow this energy to flow into you for a few moments.

Balance your will

with strength by trying

the following steps...

Step 1:

Focus and centering

Chapter 3

Focus

You're searching for your mind
Don't know where to start
Can't find the key
To fit the lock on your heart
You think you know
But you're never quite sure...
            —Ozzy Osborne

During a busy day we are constantly bombarded by a variety of demands, decisions and deadlines. The more we mentally focus on what needs to be done, the more overwhelmed we feel. These days, we tend to be a highly mentally-focused society. When stress, pain or crises arise, it seems safer to confront a problem with a mental approach rather than deal with the emotional and physical reactions to it. However, in doing this, we cut ourselves off from the broader resources available to us. **Understanding the benefits of shifting from a mental focus to a whole body awareness fundamentally changes your outlook.** You accomplish what is needed with a more subtle, yet powerful approach.

When you move your focus from the mind to another area in the body, something powerful happens. Your mind releases control, and inner and outer senses located throughout the body are immediately available. You rediscover your instincts and insight. This whole body approach not only increases your awareness, but you also process information faster than when you rely solely on the overworked mind. Imagine coming home with a new computer with a variety of programs and options. If you don't take time to familiarize yourself

27

with the programs offered, but use only a few, you won't benefit from its full potential.

Similarly, keeping your focus on the mind limits your ability to fully experience and understand what is happening around you. **However, as soon as you shift your focus from the mind, your awareness automatically expands.** You then have access to senses and insights you innately possess and can utilize them to their full potential.

Since your body's natural state is to work together, changing to a whole body approach enables you to confront problems in a healthier and more rational way. With increased awareness of your body, you'll take better care of it; in turn, it will better support you.

Centering

At the start of a busy day, we find ourselves off and running. From morning till evening, we rush here and there, make appointments and phone calls, up to our elbows in paperwork and lists. We chase after what we think we need to accomplish; although the faster we run, the further away completion seems. By the end of the day, we have not taken time to enjoy life.

Fortunately, there is a better, saner way to start your day. Try shifting your focus as you begin the day. **A powerful place to refocus is at the middle of your chest—your heart center.** Throughout your body, you have inner instincts and senses waiting to be activated. These senses work together to absorb and process the information around you. The advantage to this shift in focus is that all parts of your psyche work together to find solutions, instead of just your overworked mind. Meet life with a whole body approach and your awareness increases. With your body more relaxed, you complete tasks at a saner pace. **An added bonus is you harness the universal law of attraction.** The simple act of sitting in your calm center slows you down enough to become part of life's flow. When you center in the moment, you attract what you need—such as finding the right treatment or doctor, locating the closest parking space or recognizing opportunities you otherwise might have missed. **A simple way to shift from head to heart is to place your hand on the middle of your chest and focus there.** This gives your mind a break and aligns you with your heart center, so you experience the power of the perfect moment.

A heart-centered focus has more than one benefit. When you focus at your heart and express yourself from there, personal interactions are more meaningful. No matter who you are dealing with—family, friends, coworkers or the public in general, speaking from your heart allows you to express yourself from a neutral place. This eliminates unhealthy patterns of communication. Mental battles take place in your head, power trips happen directly below your rib cage, and heated emotional exchanges in your gut. Speak from your heart and your tone and intent automatically change, you align with your personal truth, and people know you care. You disengage from old patterns and conflicts, open new avenues for communication and resolve past issues.

Communication from the heart makes presentations more effective. Standing in front of coworkers or a room full of strangers is a stressful experience. You  reach some of the audience with a mental focus, others with an emotional appeal and still others with a powerful approach. You reach everyone with a heart-centered presentation, because you are centered and aligned with all parts of the self.

A substance abuse counselor says: "When I come from my heart center, I feel less fearful and am able to express myself more clearly and be more assertive while communicating with clients and staff."

Centering Technique

Key Word: "Center"
Sit back, relax and experience the flow.

~Shift your focus from head to heart by placing your hand in the middle of your chest.

~Gently press on your chest, as you take a deep breath into your abdomen. Hold for five seconds and as you breathe out, release any doubts, fears, stress or pain that interfere with attracting what you need.

~Say the key word, **"Center,"** out loud from your heart center. As you focus there, the universal law of attraction engages. You are now part of the flow and can attract what you need.

Quick Version: Place your hand on your chest and breathe deeply into your abdomen. Hold for five seconds and breathe out any fears, doubts, stress or pain. Say the key word, **"Center,"** out loud.

Communication Technique

~During a difficult conversation, pay attention to the areas in your body that feel stressed or uncomfortable. Notice where your words are emanating from—your mind, emotions and power.

~Place your hand on the middle of your chest and continue conversing from there. As you speak from your heart center, your personal truth and insight automatically engage. The conversation improves as all parts of you align.

Stress & Pain Release Technique
Key Word: "Center" and breathe

~Close your eyes and shift your focus from head to heart by placing one hand on the center of your chest. Say **"Center,"** out loud from there.

~Notice how your chest is feeling. Is it tight, stressed, in pain or uncomfortable? If it feels tense, try the following breathing technique. Press gently on your chest and breathe into your abdomen. Hold for five seconds. As you breathe out, release any stress, pain or tension. Feel yourself sinking into peace and relaxation.

~Next, move your focus to your stomach. How does this area feel? If there is tension, stress, pain or anxiety, place two fingers on this area and gently press, using the same method. Use this technique to release stress and pain from the neck, shoulders, back, arms or legs.

Tips for specific areas: For back pain, place a rolled-up hand towel under your back. For arm pain, hold a tennis ball in one hand while pressing on pain area with two fingers. For leg or knee pain, place a tennis ball under one foot while pressing on pain area with two fingers. Firmly grasp shoulders with hands for stress or pain release.

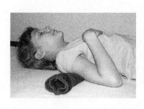   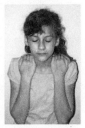

Quick Version: Take a few moments during your day to check in with your body. Use this technique to release stress and pain, increase body awareness and regain a sense of well-being.

Now that you have gained

whole-body awareness

and engaged the

universal law of attraction...

Step 2:

Inner core

Chapter 4

Inner Core

Whatever is at the center of our life will be the source
of our security, guidance, wisdom and power.
—Stephen Covey

Have you ever experienced a time when everything around you was in total chaos? The more you tried to remedy the situation, the worse it became. When life is unmanageable, we try to find a quick solution. However, when we react this way, we miss the point of the whole experience. Often upheavals in life happen to make way for new beginnings and change what is obsolete. Clinging to old patterns prevents growth. If we resist change to keep the status quo, we miss important opportunities that life offers. Now is the time to view the situation from a different perspective.

Adversity challenges you to look within and become more creative and adaptable in finding solutions. In doing this, you are forced to deal with aspects of yourself not yet developed. At first these challenges seem like roadblocks in your path—and they may stay a while.

When stress or pain strikes, go within and find the quiet, safe place that everyone possesses, your inner core and calm center. Taking time to connect with the core separates you from the chaos long enough to discover the clarity needed to resolve dilemmas like finding the right pain or stress treatment or solution, focusing on communication or finding a quiet spot to rest and regroup.

You can compare your inner core to a lighthouse shining its bright beam, guiding ships to safety on turbulent seas. Your inner core is always there, illuminating the way to your inner strength and security.

Light up the inner core and watch life become synchronistic and flow. Your core provides enough trust and confidence for any encounter.

Where is the inner core located? It runs from the top of the head to the base of the spine. Your inner core is your true self, who understands your deepest desires and holds your highest potential. Connecting with your core is experiencing the calm eye of a hurricane. It separates you from stress, pain, fear and doubt. **Engaging the inner core creates a neutral boundary between you and the chaos, giving you time to regroup.** Your core is the fabric that weaves  together your body, emotions and mind. Once these parts integrate and are infused with core energy, they instinctively work together in a balanced manner. Simply put, when we separate from our core, fear and doubt dominate. As we align with our core, we feel confident, supported and become an integral part of life.

A computer network technician instructor who regularly uses the core exercise during classes says: "I deal with sixty students a day who are new to this profession. In their excitement to learn, they often repeat the same questions. When I find myself feeling frustrated, I take a moment to connect with my core. I am able to respond to their questions in a more polite and appropriate way."

A natural therapist who gives health assessments based on acupuncture points and muscle testing explains: "Before greeting clients, I engage my inner core. Doing this creates a trust within me. I find myself guided to the problem areas, and I can help them attain their natural state of health and well-being."

Most people underestimate the power of just *being*. We live in such an aggressive and busy society, it seems foreign to take a few moments to connect with our core. When we take the time to align with our core, life's flow is felt and utilized. The inner core is a most powerful place to reside, one we should visit often.

Inner Core Technique

Key Phrase: "Center-Core"
Sit back, relax and experience—everything flows to you.

~Close your eyes and shift your focus from head to heart by placing one hand on the middle of your chest.

~Focus for a moment on your heart, the entrance to your core. Say the key word, **"Center,"** out loud from your heart. This is a signal for your conscious self to let go and be led.

~Then say, **"Core,"** out loud from your heart. This engages your inner core. Take a deep breath and hold it for five seconds. As you breathe out, sink into your inner core, while core energy neutralizes anxiety, stress and pain.

~Take a few moments to experience the calm of your inner core. As your inner and outer balance is restored, you feel confident, vibrant and part of life's flow.

Quick Version: Place your hand at your heart and say, **"Center,"** then **"Core,"** out loud from there. Take a breath and as you breathe out, feel inner core light surround you. Sit for a few moments to align with life's flow. Then go on your way, knowing you'll attract what you need.

Core-to-Core Communication

~During conversations, remember to speak from your inner core, your place of strength and personal truth. Not only do you present your best self, you engage the other person's core, whether they realize it or not. Conversations improve and communication is clear.

Now that you have

engaged your inner core...

Step 3:

Intention

Chapter 5

Intention

Live with intention
Walk to the edge
Continue to learn
Play with abandon
Choose with no regret
Laugh, do what you love
Live as if this is all there is.
—Marianne Radmacher-Hershey

When starting any new venture, whether it is a job or career, most of us are full of optimism. We choose our occupations for a variety of reasons—challenge, aptitude, pleasure, money, luck, necessity or to contribute to society. Our intentions are as lofty as rising to the top of the corporate ladder or as simple as earning enough to pay the bills.

Daily goals and intentions are useful in all aspects of life and are an important component of every day. They allow us to prioritize, stay inspired and focused. Long-term goals or intentions help us see the big picture and stay on track with the knowledge that, if we persevere in our daily goal, our efforts will eventually pay off.

Since most of us have to work, enjoying what we do for a living makes a big difference in our desire to get out of bed in the morning. Why? Being in a career that inspire and fulfill us makes life richer.

Some of us are lucky enough to find a profession we truly enjoy, while others are still searching. Either way, we need to set goals in life. We all have a basic need to improve and better ourselves, whether it's materially, emotionally, mentally or spiritually.

Writing down goals, posting them in a conspicuous place, focusing on them or repeatedly saying them are a few methods that often help us achieve them. Yet sometimes goals take years to manifest or never materialize at all. There are several reasons for this. First, as a mentally focused society, we try to figure things out logically. As we set intentions or goals, we consciously hold them too tightly with our mind and will. We are also surrounded by stress and negative energy, whether it is our own or someone else's. Consequently, our goals are affected by whatever fears, doubts or negative emotions surround us.

Another approach to achieving your goals is to place them in their rightful place—the heart center. The word *intention* begins with the syllable *in* which means within. The heart center is where your insight, instincts and personal truth reside. Speaking your intention out loud from your inner core changes a mental thought into your personal truth that manifests quickly in the physical world.

This collaboration between you and your core is powerful. Unlike your conscious self, the inner core has no preconceived ideas about your intention and does not limit the way it manifests. **When you say your intention or goal out loud, both your inner core and intuition respond, along with the universal law of attraction.** Sit quietly for a few moments, allowing the intention to soak into your inner core. Then go on your way with the assurance you'll attract what you need to achieve your goal, since it is now part of you.

Setting a goal or an intention at the start of a hectic day makes total sense. Depending on the day, you may need to draw on your inner strength to help with balance, patience, organization, adaptability or trust. At other times, attracting more concrete goals such as money, a job, housing or a relationship are the priority. Simply choose an intention and say it out loud from your core. Since the goal or intention is expressed out loud, your words resonate with your personal truth and therefore manifest quickly in the physical world.

Use the power of intention to release stress and pain. Chronic stress or pain blocks your ability to attract what you need. Blocked energy in or around you affects your goals and intentions. Emotional or mental responses regarding your health also complicate matters. You may unconsciously be holding onto stress or pain. Pay attention to your words. Do they express resignation regarding your current condition? Your core transcends the blocks and barriers created by the mind and emotions, leading to a healing solution.

A saleswoman of many years states: "Being successful in this competitive field takes a lot of time and effort. In the past when I was tired or stressed, I would project too much energy towards my clients, which would tend to put them off. Now, as I begin the day setting my intentions in my heart, I attract what I need, my interactions with my clients have improved, and my sales have increased."

A perfect example of the power of intention happened to me on New Year's Eve, 2000. I had self-published my first book earlier that same year and decided to set an intention to write for a publishing company and be paid up front this time around. I made it a two-fold intention, adding that I wanted to travel more. At midnight, I set the intentions. On January 8th of the new year, I received a phone call from my agent, Ellen, saying that a woman from Random House UK had contacted her. They liked my first book and wanted to offer me a book deal. Ellen told me this hardly ever happens in the publishing world and that whatever the subject was, I should accept. The first part of my intention manifested. My book had also been published that year in Germany. Ironically, that same day I received an e-mail from a man asking me to be part of an intuitive conference in Germany. As it turned out, the conference never materialized, since the promoter couldn't raise enough money. The good news is the book deal came through. If I had taken the time to travel that year, it would have been impossible to finish the book. *Intuition: The Key to Divination* was published in 2002.

To a certain extent, we create our own reality. Unfortunately, a majority of the time it is done unconsciously with little thought to how conditions and situations affect us.

Since thoughts are more powerful than you realize, consider your options wisely and aim for the highest good. Set an intention in your heart and become a conscious creator, enlisting the help of your inner core and utilizing life's flow. Pick a goal or intention that you want to attract into your life and try the following technique.

Intention Technique

Key Phrase: "Center-Core-(Intention)-Expand"
When you sit back, relax and experience—everything flows to you.

~Close your eyes and shift your focus from head to heart by placing one hand on the middle of your chest.

~Focus on your chest and say the key word, **"Center,"** out loud from your heart. This is your signal to let go of control and experience the quiet within. Next, engage your inner core by saying, **"Core,"** out loud slowly.

~Pick a goal or intention that you want to attract. Say it out loud from your heart center. Some intentions are: **patience, openness, adaptability, organization, stress or pain release, prosperity, balance, humor, integrity, perseverance, joy, a car, a job, a date or a vacation.**

~Sit quietly for a few moments, allowing the intention to soak into your core.

~Say, **"Expand,"** out loud from your heart center. Then go on your way, with the assurance you'll attract what you need to achieve your goal since it is now a part of you.

Quick Version: Place your hand at your heart center, and say your key words, **"Center-Core,"** out loud slowly from there. Say your intention out loud, followed by, **"Expand."**

Make a list of the day's priorities. Place the list on your heart center, focus there and say your key words. Go on your way, knowing you'll complete your list—with the help of life's flow.

Now that you have an

understanding of intention...

Step 4:

Increase your energy flow

Chapter 6

Energy

There is a muscular energy in sunlight
corresponding to the spiritual energy of the wind.
—**Annie Dillard**

To keep up with today's fast pace, we push our physical body beyond its limits, depleting its energy supply. Consequently, we turn to artificial stimuli for help, using caffeine, nicotine, drugs, alcohol or adrenaline—anything except what is free and always available, our natural energy flow. This is the fuel our body needs throughout the day. Running on this energy is not new, after all our body was designed to utilize it. **As children, we naturally tapped into this energy source; we felt connected to the earth, trusted the universe and were part of life's flow.**

When your body runs on artificial stimuli, it interrupts the energy flow and works for only a limited amount of time. Drawing on this type of energy is comparable to homes powered by gas, electricity or coal. Although these power sources are reliable, there is a definite downside to them. They use the earth's limited resources and come with a monthly bill. Similarly, when your body is pushed beyond its limits and you turn to artificial stimuli to keep going, although you don't pay a monthly bill, down the road you may end up paying lots of medical bills.

Utilizing your natural energy flow as your power source is comparable to homes relying on wind and solar power—free and inexhaustible energy resources from nature. With these resources, there is no energy depletion and the power source is free.

It makes better sense to increase your energy by utilizing two free and renewable resources: earth and universal energy.

Earth Energy

Earth energy is calm, dense energy originating from the earth. It enters the body through the feet and flows through you, increasing body awareness. This energy nourishes the physical body. Whether you work indoors or out, you may be too busy to connect with the earth properly. Consequently, you won't receive the energy your body needs. Earth energy neutralizes stress, pain, tension and anxiety and releases it into the ground. This energy calms the body, making it feel safe and secure. The key word for earth energy is "**Trust.**"

Universal Energy

Universal energy is a light airy energy that enters the body through the crown of the head. As it flows through you, it transforms blocked energy into fluid energy. It works together with earth energy, releasing stress, pain and trauma into the ground. In turn, you feel lighter, inspired, energized and adaptable. The key word for universal energy is "**Flow.**"

Mixing Energies

Earth energy feeds and supports the physical body, providing the fuel your body needs on a regular basis. Universal energy supports the psyche and increases the energy needed to "go with the flow" and adapt. As the two energies meet, they provide the balance needed for the day. Both energies fuel your inner core and engage your insight. **The best way to engage these two energies is to spend time sitting on the ground.** This allows your body to relax and release the "fight or flight" response that cuts off the natural energy flow.

Universal Energy

Earth Energy

Energy Imbalances

An imbalance of earth or universal energy affects your ability to cope with stress and pain, meet your basic needs, achieve goals or be aware of your body's needs. **An imbalance of energies is common in most people.**

Earth Energy Imbalance

If you are someone with a weak earth energy connection and a stronger universal energy connection, you deal with stress or pain by partially leaving your body. With your focus elsewhere and a weak earth support, you often experience spacey, out of body feelings. Awareness of your body's needs is also affected. This disconnect causes all sorts of problems, adversely affecting your ability to accomplish tasks or realize goals.

Ideas are forthcoming, but it is difficult to take the next step—giving them a practical and physical form. Since focus tends to leave in tense situations and your body is not supported by earth energy, it is harder to attract what you need. A job, money to pay bills or a roof over your head are necessities that don't come naturally for people with a lack of earth energy.

In the words of a woman dealing with chronic fatigue syndrome and hepatitis: "Connecting with earth and universal energy on a regular basis has helped me stabilize my body, improved my physical stamina and return to work. Added bonuses are less mental fatigue, using my intuition during my workday and the awareness to know when I am expending too much energy toward others."

Universal Energy Imbalance

If you are strongly connected to the earth but have a weak universal connection, you tend to stay in your body when stress or pain strikes. Because of the weak connection with universal energy, your body feels like the safer place. However, when dealing with pain or stress, you cope by building walls around you. With a strong connection to the earth, you usually prosper in the physical world, although you may feel blocked regarding your purpose and potential. A stronger universal connection allows you to release stress and pain while promoting inspiration and adaptability.

These are just two examples of energy imbalances. Since everyone is unique, people at various times in their lives have either of these imbalances or a combination of both. What is important to remember is this—when you strengthen both connections, your energy flow increases, you feel balanced and secure enough to align with your potential and purpose.

From an artist, art teacher and interior designer: "With the variety of jobs I do, I find myself wearing many hats. I was teaching a multitude of art classes, working with a diverse population that included independent-study and at-risk students. My busy schedule was compounded when I was diagnosed with an extremely rare form of cancer. As I was hit with this news, I felt detached from my body and my center, wondering whether I would be around in the immediate future. By connecting with earth and universal energy and relying on the earth, I found the strength to survive the ensuing treatments. These energies calmed my body enough that I was able to reclaim my career and align with my inner self. It has been twelve years since this roller coaster began. I now work part-time with a more manageable schedule and am cancer-free."

You make the choice. Continually depleting your body's energy resources ultimately leads to stress and disease, whereas running on a blend of both energies calms and energizes your physical body, allowing you to plug into life's flow. Pain and stress once again can release into the ground. And don't forget, there is no monthly bill!

A woman dealing with fibromyalgia for the last 16 years states: "During Gina's course, I learned new ways to clear my pain as well as limit my stress, and change how I react to both. After using the energy flow technique, I was amazed at the energy flowing through my body. One exciting benefit that came directly from the course was opening up my creative side, which led me to start up my own photography business."

Integrate the 4 steps and key words

for the remaining exercises in this book...

Step 1: Shift your focus from head to your heart by placing your hand on the middle of your chest. Focus there and say the key word, "**Center**," out loud. Your heart center is the doorway to your inner core and personal truth. Let go of control and allow yourself to be led.

Step 2: Say the key word, "**Trust**," out loud to increase the earth energy flow and release stress and pain into the ground.

Step 3: Say the key word, "**Flow**," out loud to increase the universal energy flow and align with your purpose and potential.

Step 4: Say the key word, "**Core**," out loud to engage your inner instincts and senses.

The following techniques are designed to increase your energy flow and release any trapped stress or pain throughout the body.

A mother of three boys has this to say: "As a long time sufferer of migraine headaches, I can tell you firsthand that by using the stress and pain release techniques, I've drastically reduced the frequency of my headaches, as well as making the need for prescription medication almost non-existent. I also found the techniques valuable in controlling anxiety. In the past, I experienced anxiety attacks which were so bad, they caused me to leave an event or social gathering. By using these techniques, I found I can control the attacks within minutes."

Energy Flow Technique

Key Phrase: "Center-Trust-Flow-Core"

~Start the day with this exercise. Close your eyes and shift your focus by placing one hand at your heart center. Say, **"Center,"** out loud from there.

~Rub your hands together briskly for a few moments. Place your hands a foot apart, while facing each other. Sense the energy between them. Notice whether the energy is tingly, warm, cool, flowing, heavy or magnetic.

~Next, increase your earth energy flow by saying, **"Trust,"** out loud from your heart. Feel the energy change between your hands. Earth energy flows in through your feet, fills your body and provides a secure base.

~Increase your universal energy flow by saying, **"Flow,"** out loud from your heart. Again, notice the energy change. Universal energy flows in through your crown. Allow both energies to mix and create the balance needed for the day.

~Energize your inner core with both energy sources by saying the key word, **"Core,"** out loud from your heart. Take a breath and allow your inner core light to expand around you.

At times your body needs more earth or universal energy. When this occurs, allow this energy to flow for a longer period of time.

Quick Version: Place your hand at your heart, focus there and say, **"Center-Core,"** out loud slowly from there. Since both earth and universal energy were established in the morning, they automatically engage. Take a breath, expanding your core energy around you.

Headache Technique

~Sit or lie back for a few moments and close your eyes. Move your focus from head to heart by placing your hand on the middle of your chest. Focus there while saying the key words, **"Center-Core,"** out loud slowly from your heart.

~Place one hand over your forehead (to calm the mental chatter) and the other hand at the base of your skull (your "fight or flight" area).

~Say the key word, **"Forward."** This releases the band of will and allows the pain to come forward and intensify.

~Say the key word, **"Lavender,"** from your heart. Lavender is a calm, healing energy that cools and absorbs trapped pain or stress within the body. Take a few moments to allow the lavender color to work.

~Next, say the key word, **"Release,"** out loud from your heart. Feel the pain leave through your crown. Repeat the process a few times as needed.

Quick Version: Lie down, close your eyes and place one hand over your forehead. Place the other hand on the base of your skull. Focus at your heart and say, **"Forward,"** out loud from your heart. Soften and absorb the pain by saying, **"Lavender."** Say, **"Release,"** out loud from your heart, allowing the pain to leave.

This exercise relieves headaches, mental fatigue and insomnia.

Pain Release Technique

Key Phrase: "Center-Core-Forward-Orange-Release"

~Move your focus from head to heart by placing one hand on the middle of your chest. Focus and say, **"Center- Core,"** out loud slowly.

~Choose an area of your body that is in pain. Put slight pressure on this area with two fingers. If the pain is in a hard-to-reach area, see below for instructions.

~Say the key word, **"Forward."** This releases the band of will and allows the pain to come forward and intensify.

~Say the key word, **"Orange,"** from your heart. Orange is a warm, healing energy that absorbs trapped pain or stress and enables the area to accept a healing. Take a few moments to allow the orange to work.

~Next, say the key word, **"Release,"** out loud from your heart. Feel the pain leave through your feet, hands or crown. Repeat the process a few times if needed. For chronic pain, use this technique daily.

Tips for specific areas: For back pain, place a rolled-up hand towel under your back. For arm pain, hold a tennis ball in one hand while pressing on pain area with two fingers. For leg or knee pain, place a tennis ball under one foot while pressing on pain area with two fingers. Firmly grasp shoulders with hands for stress or pain release.

   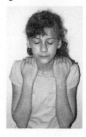

Now that you have

increased your energy flow...

Find out about

grounding

Chapter 7

Grounding

*The best remedy for those who are afraid, lonely or unhappy
is to go outside somewhere where they can be quiet,
alone with the heavens, nature and God.
Because only then does one feel that all is
as it should be, amidst the simple beauty of nature.
I firmly believe that nature brings solace in all troubles.*
—Anne Frank

Our body is an incredible machine. Wake it up in the wee hours of the morning, fill it full of coffee, shove it out the door and off to work it goes. During a busy workday, we drag our body around behind us, stressing it with what seems like a million phone calls, meetings, and deadlines. Halfway through the day, when it is exhausted, we ply it with caffeine, aspirin and fast food, wondering why it can't keep up. When you think about it, the physical body does an amazing job coping with today's fast pace, although sometimes it's pushed too far.

In the past, life was only about survival. People spent most days hunting and foraging for food which kept them in top physical condition. They listened to their body's instinctual responses, because often their life depended on them. Since the majority of time was spent outdoors, people were naturally grounded and connected to the earth, working within life's rhythms.

By contrast, in modern times, we spend most of the working day inside—surrounded by noise, stress and hectic schedules. As life's pace quickens, we lose the ability to stay in touch with our body's natural responses and needs. As we increasingly ignore our body's signals, we create artificial barriers to cope. These barriers include weight gain, alcohol, cigarettes, drugs and other addictions. Unfortunately, these blocks not only affect our relationship with our body, but also our interactions with others. We start relating to the physical body as separate from us and cease listening to its signals when it's tired, rundown, stressed or in pain. As a result, it is pushed beyond its limits and shuts down. A majority of people today are unaware they are walking around in a continual state of "fight or flight." As time goes on, the natural energy flow is reduced. Consequently, weight, depression, mental fatigue, stress and pain can become trapped in the body.

When the physical body is on overload, it resists everything and is slower to embrace change than you are. As it encounters too much stress or pain—any change, whether positive or negative, is viewed as a danger. Since your body is not cognitive, it does not respond to reason. Its main job is to protect you. You may be excited about a promotion, job change or a move to a different location. Even so, your body may not be. If it is under too much stress, it may use sickness, weight gain, even a breakdown to resist any type of change and protect itself.

When your body is distressed, your focus is more likely to leave. In turn, you experience that spacey or disconnected feeling. Grounding is renewing your connection with the earth. Start the day this way and feel supported and connected. In doing so, you respond to change or stress in a healthier way. Moreover, grounding gives you  a heightened awareness of your body's needs. Many people notice their pain leaving when they take time to ground with the earth.

A woman with chronic back pain had this to say about grounding: "I took the stress and pain class and was looking forward to learning the pain release technique, since I have intense lower lumbar pain. As we tried the grounding exercise, I felt calmer and my back pain immediately lessened."

Grounding and Exercise

Although exercise is a great way to release stress and stay clear mentally and emotionally, it is important to balance workouts with enough time connecting with the ground. Like anything else, exercise can be overdone and overused. **Sometimes you force yourself to exercise, when what your body really needs is a break.** As the physical body is continually pushed beyond its limits, it triggers a survival response. When this happens, the body protects itself by holding on to stress and resisting any will-driven push to perform. When mind and will drive the body, ignoring its signals, the end result may be injury or chronic disease.

Before I start my exercise routine, I take a moment to press on the bottom of both feet and hold them for a minute. This increases the energy flow and allows stress and pain to release during my workout. When I finish, I repeat this technique. I find the positive results of my workout stay with me longer.

At times, rigorous exercise routines result in tight muscles that cut down on the energy flow in the body. **An easy way to relieve tight calf or thigh muscles is to place tennis balls under both thighs or calves for five minutes.** If these muscles still feel blocked, place one ball under a calf or thigh and another ball under the foot of 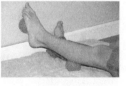 the same leg. Position the foot against a wall, using the Pain Release Technique. Do the same for the opposite leg. This relieves tight muscles, while increasing the energy flow through the legs and out the feet.

During the day, make sure to spend some quality time sitting on the ground. If there is a park near work, a small section of grass or a tree nearby, you can regain your sense of composure and help your body rebalance by grounding with the earth. The reward is that your mind, emotions and body work in unison. Subsequently, you instinctively know when to exercise and when to take a break.

During the winter I lie in front of the fire in the yoga position, Child Pose, and imagine myself sinking into the ground. A hot bath also works well in the winter.

Grounding and Trauma

Grounding is essential before undergoing any medical procedure. Since your body's job is to protect you, it may regard an operation or other medical procedure as a danger and offer resistance. Instead, enlist your body's cooperation and help in healing by grounding it before the procedure. In doing so, the body has the support of the earth and can "go with the flow" instead of resorting to survival mode.

Similarly, a traumatic experience leaves you feeling disconnected from your body. Grounding calms your body, helping it feel safe by providing it with the earth's support. The increased energy flow that grounding provides helps the body recover quickly, releasing the imprint of the trauma as it heals.

This technique came in handy a few years ago when I was working on the river during a high-water season. A third of the way down the river, my crew and I noticed a woman clinging to a tree in midstream. Another guide and I made it to shore and climbed upriver directly across from her. We were able to toss her a throwbag and pull her to shore. She seemed distraught and traumatized, even when safely ashore. I asked if I could do a calming exercise with her. She agreed and I took both of her hands and grounded her body with the earth. As a result, she calmed down and felt better. As an added bonus, I was more focused and calm as well.

If someone you know is upset or not feeling well, do a grounding exercise with them. Hold their hands in yours or press the middle of the bottom of their feet. Then try the Grounding Technique on page 60. As the energies flow through your hands into theirs, focus at your heart center. You'll both feel more centered and rejuvenated.

A massage therapist's anecdote: "I recently had surgery to remove a brain tumor. The stress and pain release techniques I used prior to the surgery helped turn a frightening situation into a positive experience. While I was hooked on monitors and in intensive care, my husband held my feet at certain points using the manual grounding technique. During a time of great physical discomfort, the simple act of holding my feet was so soothing. It was also comforting to my family to see the proof on the monitors, especially at a time when I couldn't communicate with them in other ways. I can't imagine going through that process without the coping tools that Gina provided for my family and me."

Grounding Living Spaces

After working with energy for the last twenty years, I understand the importance of grounding and clearing areas that are constantly filled with our emotions and energy. Homes, offices,  cars—any living spaces we inhabit, collect energy from our interactions. Depending on these encounters, this energy may feel light and uplifting or heavy and debilitating. A client once told me she hated to enter her office in the morning. The minute she walked in the room, she felt drained and tired. Her job involved overseeing a large firm with lots of stressful interactions among a variety of people; apparently the emotionally charged energy seemed to hang in the air. However, when she started to ground and clear the energy in her office on a daily basis, she noticed the difference right away and felt better at work.

An environmental designer and feng shui practitioner notes: "The grounding exercise has become an essential part of my business. I make sure to ground myself in the morning to give me focus and clarity during my workday. I then ground and clear the office, sharing this valuable tool with my clients."

On a personal note, when my daughter was little, she was afraid of the dark. She made up a little rhyme before she went to bed to help her feel safe during the night. Over the years, I used her rhyme in my courses with good results. It goes like this, "Mother Earth, ground me. White light surround me." Such an expression of grounding can make us all feel more secure and connected to the earth and the universe. I modify it to clear any living space that is full of stuck energy. "Mother Earth ground this home, office or car. White light clear this home, office or car."

An applicant recalls: "A few years ago I had an interview for a part-time job. After a few minutes of waiting, I got up and left. It wasn't fear of the interview that made me leave, even though I did feel nervous about it. The receptionist was friendly enough, and the office decor was pleasant. Instead, what made me uncomfortable was the atmosphere. Sitting there, I felt suffocated by the energy of the office. I couldn't imagine working in a place with that kind of smothering feeling surrounding me. I now know that I can change the atmosphere of any living space by grounding it."

Imagine the difference grounding makes when you clear the energy in your living and working spaces on a daily basis.

Grounding and Animals

Animals also need grounding at times and are a lot easier to ground than humans. On one occasion some good friends of mine had just come home from vacation to find their dog, Rocky, out of sorts. Rocky was howling a lot and resisted going outside, in contrast to his usual behavior. The next morning, he was still acting the same way, so they took him to their vet. Since the vet found nothing physically wrong with him, they decided something must have scared him while they were gone. Together, they grounded him with earth and universal energy. As a result, Rocky calmed down and was soon acting like himself again.

A few years ago, I was sitting by the river and decided to lie down on the bank to connect with the earth. No one was around other then a few Canadian geese, so I felt comfortable lying by the water. I closed my eyes and felt myself sink into the earth and started to relax.

After five minutes, I felt refreshed and decided to walk back to my house. As I started to get up, I was startled to find that the geese had moved very close and were nesting around me in a half circle three feet away. While I had been lying there, I was so connected to the earth, they hadn't realized how close they had come to me. I was so relaxed, I didn't hear them approach. This experience doesn't say much for my survival skills, but it does show when you connect with the earth, the resulting energy flow is felt by others, human or not.

When you take time in the morning to ground and increase your energy flow, people, like the geese, are drawn to you. Consequently, you attract what you need. Such grounding is important when dealing with financial concerns, work-related matters or navigating through the maze of medical issues and insurance.

The following techniques can be completed quickly and provide the necessary support during your day. Take a moment to regroup and renew your connection with the earth whenever your busy schedule throws you off balance.

Grounding Technique

Key Phrase: "Center-Core-Ground"
Remember to allow this technique to happen rather than forcing it.

~Start the day with this exercise. Close your eyes and shift your focus by placing one hand at your heart center. Say, **"Center,"** out loud from there.

~If earth and universal energy were established in the morning, they automatically engage. If not, say the key words, **"Trust-Flow,"** slowly out loud from your heart.

~Engage your inner core by saying the key word, **"Core,"** out loud from your heart. Take a deep breath and feel core energy surround you.

~Lay both hands on your lap, palms toward the ceiling and say the key word, **"Ground,"** out loud from your heart. You may experience a sinking feeling while your body connects with the earth.

Quick Version: During the day when life disrupts your grounding, use this method to engage the earth and your core while increasing your energy flow. Say the key words out loud from your heart, **"Center-Core-Ground"** or **"Mother Earth, ground me. White light surround me."** Earth and universal energy automatically engage.

Living Space Technique

Key Phrase: "Center-Core-Connect-Let go-Ground"

~Sit quietly in the living space that needs grounding and close your eyes. Shift your focus from head to heart by placing your hand on the middle of your chest. Say, **"Center,"** out loud from there.

~If earth and universal energy were established in the morning, they automatically engage. If not, say the key words, **"Trust-Flow,"** to increase your energy flow.

~Engage your inner core by saying, **"Core,"** out loud slowly from your heart.

~Raise your hands over your head with palms facing the ceiling. Say, **"Connect,"** out loud from your heart. Wait until you feel core energy in the palms of your hands. Say, **"Let go,"** out loud from your heart. Allow inner core energy to guide your hands. As they start to move on their own, they will attract any stuck energy in the room, releasing it into the ground.

Quick Version: Place your hand on the middle of your chest and say this phrase out loud, **"Center-Core-Ground"** or **"Mother Earth ground this home, office or car. White light clear this home, office or car."**

Ground yourself at the same time that you ground your living space. Simply expand your intention to include both.

Manual Grounding Approach

Sometimes your body experiences an excessive amount of stress, pain or trauma and needs a hands-on approach. Opening certain key areas in the feet and head quickly calms and releases the body from a "fight or flight" response while restoring the energy flow.

The first step in this process stabilizes the earth connection, increasing the energy flow to the body through the feet. Since there are two different methods, choose the one that is most comfortable for you. Either press firmly with two fingers on the middle of the bottom of each foot or place two tennis balls under both feet and press down firmly. Both methods increase the energy flow through the feet, simultaneously releasing stress and pain into the ground. Say the key word, **"Trust,"** out loud from your heart center to start the process. **Use the tennis ball method when studying or working on the computer. It releases stress and allows you to stay focused.**

This next step works either sitting up or lying down. However, I experience the best results when I lie down. Start by closing your eyes and placing one hand over your forehead. This relaxes the mind, which in turn releases control—along with any stress or pain in the head. Then place the opposite hand on the base of your skull, which governs the survival response. This technique relaxes both areas, allowing them to integrate and work together. Start this process by saying the key word, **"Flow,"** out loud from your heart.

Next, its time to balance the left and right sides of the body. Start by firmly grasping the top of both ears, pulling upward for 30 seconds to one minute. Then, pull down on the ear lobes for the same amount of time. Now, pull out on the middle of both ears. This technique is similar to acupressure and relieves vertigo.

The last step releases anxiety, stress or pain in and around the chest area. Place two fingers on your upper chest (see photo). This area is usually tender to the touch. Say your key word, **"Core,"** and wiggle your fingers gently for 15 seconds. Hold your fingers still for the same amount of time to stabilize the change. Repeat until stress or pain is released or soreness is relieved. This method helps with asthma.

Manual Grounding Technique

Key Phrase: "Center-Trust-Flow-Core"

~Place one hand on your heart and say, **"Center,"** out loud from there.

 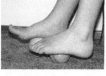 ~To increase the energy flow between your feet and your head, grasp the middle bottom of each foot or place tennis balls under both feet. Say the key word, **"Trust,"** out loud from your heart. Allow earth energy to calm and energize you for 30-60 seconds.

~Place one hand over your forehead (to calm the mental chatter) and the other hand on the base of your skull (your "fight or flight" area). Say the key word, **"Flow,"** out loud from your heart.  Allow universal energy to calm and release stress or pain in your head.

~To balance the left and right sides of the body, gently grasp the top of both ears and pull up firmly for 30 seconds to one minute (Photo A).

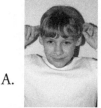

A.

B.

C.

~Gently pull on the bottom of both ear lobes for the same amount of time (Photo B). Pull out on the middle edge of both ears (Photo C).

~Place two fingers on your upper chest in areas that are tender. (see picture for placement). Say, **"Core,"** out loud from your heart and wiggle your fingers gently for 15 seconds. Hold your fingers still for the same amount of time. Repeat until soreness is gone.

Now that you have

given your body

a secure base...

Explore your

boundaries

Chapter 8

Boundaries

Don't ever take a fence down
until you know why it was put there.
—Robert Frost

In today's densely populated world, the term *boundaries* is heard more and more in our vocabulary. A busy day finds us exchanging energy with people we encounter both in person and on the phone. We unknowingly share our stress and anxiety with each other. Without a healthy boundary around us, this exchange of energy depletes the physical body, leaving us feeling drained by the end of the day.

Boundaries are essential in all areas of our lives—at work, home and play. As small children, we learned the boundaries of our parents and siblings. Later, we experienced boundaries with friends, classmates and teachers. For me, however, there was never a tangible way to set boundaries, until I began working with people's energy. As I started teaching classes, I became more sensitive and felt the energy of different boundaries. I could tell where one person's energy stopped and another person's began. **With this increased awareness, I discovered a discernible way to help others sense and establish healthy boundaries—energetically.**

A perfect example of this involved a woman in my class who had a seemingly prickly outer layer surrounding her personal space. However, beneath it was a warm, loving layer that more accurately reflected her identity. The problem was that most people reacted to her prickly outer layer. Although if they stayed around her long enough, they found she was a warm and caring person. During the class, I showed her how to ground and clear her space, expanding her inner core energy around her. This transformed her prickly outer layer into neutral energy, helping her express who she is now rather than her old defense mechanism.

Types of Boundaries

Over the years, I found that people have distinctive energies within their personal space that form their boundaries. They run the spectrum from feeling uplifting or comfortable, to feeling weak, prickly, aggressive or solid as a brick wall.

Weak or strong boundaries correspond to various personality types and situations. Furthermore, people naturally expand their boundaries when feeling good or powerful, retract them when feeling bad or use them as a defense mechanism when feeling hurt or vulnerable. **Our boundaries continuously project our thoughts and feelings, no matter how adept we are at masking them.**

People with strong energy surrounding them, not only fill their own space, but also invade the space of those around them. For example, while trying to get their point across in a conversation, these people project their energy into other people's space, causing them to feel unconsciously pushed or pressured. Although this type of boundary works in the short term, the long-term result is resentment, lack of cooperation or eventual rebellion on the receiver's part.

Giving others the space to express themselves makes a significant difference in personal relationships, clients and coworkers. Relationships improve greatly when you allow those around you to express themselves without invading their personal space.

Conversely, people with a weak boundary tend to retract their personal space close to their bodies in stressful situations. Such a reaction adversely affects behavior. For example, people who react this way have a hard time speaking up for themselves. Saying *no* to people with stronger personalities is especially difficult. However, as they learn to expand their energy, their boundary strengthens. They then feel more powerful and able to express themselves in a more assertive and healthy way.

A senior engineer's experience with boundaries: "In the past, certain clients and coworkers would consistently invade my space. By the end of the day, their energy would collect in my gut. During the course of Gina's seminar, I realized lots of people unconsciously use their energy to manipulate others. Setting healthy boundaries throughout my workday keeps me free of power games, leaving me with more energy after work."

Expanding healthy boundaries around you and speaking from your inner core transforms unhealthy energy patterns into more balanced relationships. **Remember, you can't change other people, although you can change yourself.** Surround yourself with a three-foot personal space of core energy and establish a neutral boundary that can be renewed throughout the day. Changing unhealthy patterns allows you to respond to others in a different way, inviting other people involved to do the same.

Boundaries and Health

Any area in the body continuously affected by chronic stress, pain or invasive energy, gradually weakens and becomes susceptible to health issues. If you are in a profession involving constant interaction and communication, your body's natural boundary wears down from the energy of people, cell phones, computers and a stressful lifestyle. Chronic pain also weakens the natural boundary of affected areas. Let's explore some simple techniques designed to establish healthy boundaries at work, at home and on the phone.

"Talk to the Hand"

Most people are unaware of the energy impacting them as they walk through their day. Energy interactions affect everybody's energy level, leaving them exhausted by day's end. This constant energy drain takes a huge toll on the body, leaving little energy left for pleasure. Most people don't just listen with their ears, the energy of the interaction also affects their throat, chest and stomach areas.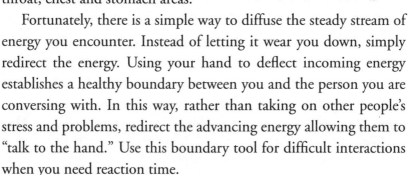

Fortunately, there is a simple way to diffuse the steady stream of energy you encounter. Instead of letting it wear you down, simply redirect the energy. Using your hand to deflect incoming energy establishes a healthy boundary between you and the person you are conversing with. In this way, rather than taking on other people's stress and problems, redirect the advancing energy allowing them to "talk to the hand." Use this boundary tool for difficult interactions when you need reaction time.

This technique calls for subtlety and discretion, since having your hand in front of another person's face is not a great way to make friends and influence people. I had a special boundary tool made as a reminder to set my boundaries during the day. It is a snazzy little ball-point pen that says on it, "Talk to the hand."

Here are a few subtle ways to redirect the energy away from your body. If you are giving a speech at a podium, allow it to become your boundary—diffusing the energy from the audience. A magazine or note pad placed on your stomach sets a boundary quickly and efficiently while deflecting the emotions and energy of others. Another method involves crossing your legs, placing one hand on your knee and imagining the other person's energy veering right or left as it meets your personal space.

Redirecting the stream of energy from you does not mean you don't care. You are establishing a healthy boundary around you with built-in reaction time while changing unhealthy communication patterns.

Phone Boundaries

In almost any profession, the constant ring of the phone is a major annoyance. Moreover, cellular phones have expanded communication, making you available 24 hours a day. Considering the amount of time spent on the phone, it is understandable that you cringe when the phone rings.

Even if you wear a headset or blue tooth—your ear, throat and head area are closely affected by other people's energy; more so than if your were talking to them directly. Add to this the effect of electronic devices, it is no wonder you feel drained by phone conversations. Speaker phones establish a healthy boundary; although some people on the other end of the conversation may feel uncomfortable. Fortunately, this technique works quite nicely with phone interactions. The next time you hear the phone ring, put one hand in front of you and allow the other person to "talk to the hand."

When you first begin using this technique, conversations may seem less engaging. However, with practice, you'll enjoy the interactions more without the added stress. When people blend too much on an energy level, they overload their bodies which doesn't improve anyone's attitude. The benefits are apparent when you have more energy for your personal pursuits.

Computer Boundaries

Invasive energy emanating from a computer affects the electromagnetic field surrounding the physical body. This field encircles everyone, playing a large part in keeping the body healthy. (See more about this field in Chapter 10.) Take a few moments to set a neutral boundary while turning on your computer. This boundary creates a buffer between the computer's energy and your body. Place your hand in front of the screen and notice the radiating energy. Now close your eyes, place the opposite hand at your heart center and say the key words, "**Center-Core-Expand**," out loud. You'll feel a calm energy radiating from your hand that acts as a buffer between the computer and you. Core energy diffuses the energy radiating from the screen.

As I wrote this book, I used this method and renewed my boundary every hour. Try this technique the next time you turn on your computer. You'll notice the difference in the way you feel when you take the time to set a healthy boundary.

Boundaries and Emotions

Have you ever woken in the morning feeling angry or out of sorts? You decide to ignore or repress the emotions, hoping to have a good day in spite of the way you feel. Later in the day, you notice that people you encounter seem angry and push your buttons. When an emotion is ignored or repressed, its energy still permeates your personal space, affecting not only you but also those around you.

Your personal space continuously projects your thoughts and feelings, no matter how adept you are at masking them. When you are feeling upbeat and centered, the projected emotions can positively affect interactions. Thus, if you are impatient, pushy or sad, these emotions negatively affect others. People you come in contact with feel uplifted or exhausted accordingly. Trapped emotions or mental strain that is not released or expressed will back up, eventually affecting your well-being.

What can you do if you wake up and don't feel on top of the world? There are days where you have no time to deal with intense feelings. Rather than pushing these emotions aside or repressing them, neutralize them with your core energy. Your core is the fabric with many threads woven together that integrate all parts of self. When powered by earth and potential energy, core energy neutralizes stuck emotions, distress and anxiety, releasing them into the ground.

Boundaries and Empowerment

If your job involves supervision, caretaking, counseling or teaching, you probably deal with immense responsibility, split-second decision-making, a wide range of personalities and face considerable stress. When situations seem out of hand, you resort to control as the quickest way to remedy a situation. Control seems like an easier solution than allowing others to find their own answers. Communication involves much more than just words. Body language, tone and intent also send potent messages to others. Although your intent is to empower others  by the words you choose, your energy exchange may send a different message. For example, allowing people too close in your personal space creates an unhealthy pattern of dependency and results in shouldering their burdens for them. Conversely, expanding too much energy toward people is an invasion of their personal space, leaving them feeling overpowered instead of empowered.

The more self-aware you are, the healthier your interactions will be. Setting healthy boundaries daily—knowing how to expand or retract your energy field, sends a clear message of empowerment instead of a mixed message to everyone involved. Best of all, when your personal space is clear, you experience more clarity. With increased energy, you have more patience to empower others. Instead of resorting to control which leads to dependency, power trips or conflict, why not encourage them to find their own solutions?

When communication breaks down, it's time to renew your boundaries with core energy. It is unnecessary to gauge where your boundaries are—simply take a moment to focus on your heart center and set a healthy boundary. If you are in the middle of a conversation that is heading south, place one hand on your heart center, making sure to speak your words from there. The moment you engage your inner core and speak from your personal truth, the conversation improves. Whether it's a heated emotional exchange, a power trip or a mental battle, shifting to a heart-centered approach automatically creates a more healthy exchange between you and the person involved. Having more patience and reaction time allows you to empower others to find their own solutions.

Boundaries and Pain

Anyone who has experienced chronic pain knows first hand how taxing it is on their well-being. Not only are you dealing with life's daily demands, you also juggle doctor visits, medical bills and insurance claims, along with the effects of medication. The pain and underlying stress wear down the body's natural defenses and boundaries, eventually creating more issues than the original problem.

Chronic pain adversely affects your instinctual self, sending you into a "fight or flight" response. As communication breaks down between the body, emotions and mind—pain, mental fatigue and depression become trapped between these layers.

Some people respond by retreating into themselves, simultaneously retracting their energy close to their body. This response creates a weak boundary which leaves them feeling vulnerable and low on energy. As a result, when faced with stressful situations, they find themselves overreacting emotionally or withdrawing, since their natural boundary is depleted.

Another coping mechanism involves creating walls between you and the pain or stress. This approach works for a short period. However, in the long run, the energy used to keep the walls in place is more depleting than the original distress. Brick-wall boundaries promote feelings of isolation, creating barriers between you and your healing path.

Your inner core is a strong support system which is reliable when dealing with chronic pain. It is the fabric that reconnects your body, emotions and mind. Unlike a will-based boundary, it does not trap pain and its complications. Instead, it aligns with your body's energy flow to usher stress, pain and anxiety into the ground. It is the strongest link between earth and universal energy.

Core energy establishes a healthy boundary based on strength instead of will. It neutralizes blocked energy, transforming it into flowing energy again.

An employment background investigator explains: "I was having severe thyroid problems and was told by my doctor that I might need to have surgery. My job involves working in front of a computer screen and talking on a cell phone for long periods of time. Over the next few weeks, I used the boundary techniques at work. Right away I felt the difference in my energy level. I was able to keep other people's energy from affecting my throat and dragging me down. By my next doctor's visit, I had no pain or pressure in my thyroid, so surgery wasn't necessary."

Boundary Technique

Key Phrase: "Center-Core-Expand"

~To renew your boundary during the day, shift your focus from head to heart by placing your hand at the middle of your chest. Say your key word, **"Center,"** out loud from your heart.

~Engage your core by saying your key word, **"Core,"** out loud from your heart center.

~If earth and universal energy were established in the morning, they automatically engage. If not, include the key words, **"Trust-Flow,"** to engage and increase your energy flow.

~Take a breath and as you breathe out, say the key word, **"Expand,"** out loud from your heart. Allow your core energy to surround you, setting a healthy boundary for the day.

Quick Version: When life knocks you off balance, renew your energy connections and boundary by saying, **"Center-Core-Expand,"** slowly out loud from your heart. Take a breath and as you breathe out, your core energy sets a healthy boundary.

"Talk to the Hand" Technique

Remember to allow this technique to happen rather than forcing it.

~When the phone rings, raise your hand and allow whoever is on the other end to "talk to the hand." This deflects the other person's energy to your hand and gives your throat a needed break.

~During conversations, give your body a needed break. Deflect their energy away from your body and have them "talk to the hand."

~If it's inconvenient to use your hand as a boundary, redirect their energy by imagining the other person's energy veering right or left as it meets your personal space. Place one hand on your knee to guide the energy past you while protecting your stomach area.

A magazine or note pad held up against your stomach can also be used as a quick boundary to deflect the energy of others. This redirection of energy gives your body a needed break, allowing you to enjoy the company of others—while not taking on their stress or pain.

Computer Boundary Technique

Key Phrase: "Center-Core-Expand"

~As you turn on your computer, take a few moments to set a neutral boundary. Place your hand in front of the screen and feel the energy radiating from it. Keep your hand there as you follow the next step.

~Place your other hand on the middle of your chest and focus there. Say, **"Center-Core-Expand,"** out loud slowly from your heart center.

~Feel core energy emanate from your hand. This energy creates a buffer between you and the computer. Renew this boundary hourly.

Quick Version: As you turn on your computer, place one hand on the middle of your chest and focus there. Say the key words, **"Center-Core-Expand,"** slowly out loud from your heart center.

Now that you have

practiced setting

healthy boundaries...

Get acquainted with

your speakers

Chapter 9

Speakers

Each of us is born with the potential
for the unfolding of our true self.
When you deviate from the truth,
you are interfering with the intention of something
far greater than you are—call it nature or a higher power.
As a result you develop discomfort in your body and psyche.
Therefore, anxiety may be regarded as meaningful
communication from a powerful force within you
that wants you to be yourself.

—Joyce Ashley

Technology has advanced so rapidly in the last few years that we are truly in the age of information. Computers, cell phones, the internet, e-mail and texting have revolutionized our life, making us more productive. However, these advances have placed additional demands on an already busy lifestyle.

Communication available at our fingertips has changed our nine-to-five workday, enabling us to be available morning, noon and night. Although this development is often financially lucrative, it takes a huge toll on the physical body. Changing to a whole body awareness is one great way to stay sane and keep up with the demands of today's world. When you make this shift, not only do you access all five outer senses, you also engage your inner senses and instincts. **The next step is acquainting yourself with the seven major energy centers or chakras in the body.** Their main purpose is to send, receive and process information. An understanding of their location and how they work is like having a road map of the body, providing you with increased awareness and insight.

Energy centers are shaped like cones or small speakers. These speakers are connected to the inner core. They constantly input and output information, expressing who you are and how you feel to those around you. At the same time, they absorb and process information from the immediate environment, helping you make sense of what is happening around you. When they work properly and in unison, they do so with such amazing speed and efficiency that you may be unaware that they are functioning.

If your speakers are healthy and in alignment, they work together as a whole, giving a clear picture of your present circumstances. However, when bombarded by too much stress, pain or stimulation, the input you receive is distorted or unclear. As a result, the output you send won't reflect your message clearly. This misinformation causes all sorts of problems—such as misunderstandings or overreactions to people or situations.

Our energy centers or speakers begin to form when we are infants. They are shaped by the many different experiences we have in childhood. Intense experiences overwhelm the newly formed speakers, causing weak areas in them as we grow. Later, these weak areas inhibit our ability to cope with life's challenges. However, in the bigger picture, these weak areas provide opportunities for growth. As adults, we may face similar patterns or issues that reflect the original trauma we first experienced. If we recognize and change these patterns, we'll manifest more clearly what we desire in life.

Acquaint yourself with your speakers and increase your understanding of where and how these patterns and limitations affect you. Illness, pain and stress are all catalysts that command your attention. Using the information your speakers provide allows you to quickly find healing solutions while recognizing the underlying message.

Speakers Diagram

7. Crown Speaker

6. Mental Speaker

5. Throat Speaker

4. Heart Speaker

3. Power Speaker

2. Emotional Speaker

1. Survival Speaker

1. Survival Speaker

When something as traumatic as losing your home, job or relationship occurs, it feels like someone just pulled the rug out from under you. This analogy is an accurate description of what is happening to you on an energy level. In this situation, sudden changes affect your most basic needs, giving rise to feelings of panic and disconnectedness.

The survival speaker is associated with the adrenal gland and is located between the ovaries in women—at the base of the spine in men. This speaker faces downward, since it is the main link between your physical body and the earth. If your survival speaker is partially blocked, you will feel uncertain or fearful about the world as a whole. Feeling insecure and unsupported affects your ability to meet your basic needs. Trauma, intense experiences or an unstable upbringing causes a weak connection in this speaker, disrupting your connection with the earth. This leaves you feeling ungrounded and unsupported, affecting your personal life and work performance.

Up through the age of 7, you are absorbing pertinent survival information from your parents or primary caregivers, whether or not the information is accurate. The survival speaker is affected by faulty programming throughout childhood. The environment you grow up in and your own connection with the earth also influences early survival programming. This input may or may not give you the support you need to cope with adversity—making you feel either safe or unsafe in this world.

From ages 8 to 18, your own experiences are filtered through this parental programming. All these experiences add to this storehouse of information or misinformation. If you lived in a perfect world, you could consciously sift through your parental programming, storing only valid information and discarding the rest.

This filtering process happens on the subconscious level. You may one day realize you are running on faulty programming that has nothing to do with you or how you perceive the world as an adult. Such misinformation creates limitations and blind spots in your life. As an example, your parents may have grown up in the great depression. Consequently, you are obsessed with financial security. In reality, you have financial security, but it never seems like enough.

Pain or injury occurring around the base of the spine may be the catalyst for examining what constitutes security and support in your life. The following anecdote offers insight into pain and its underlying issues.

> An art director states: "Years ago I was involved in an auto accident in which my family's van careened down a mountainside. Thankfully, a small cedar tree caught the van, preventing it from ending up at the bottom of a ravine. After that, whenever I rode in a car, I experienced an intense feeling of vulnerability and felt out of control. Gina showed me how to use the speaker technique to release the pain and imprint of the accident. As I was releasing this trauma, I uncovered a connected feeling I experienced when I was six years old that involved my mother's nervous breakdown. Feelings of abandonment and loss of control were related to both events. Using this technique allowed me to heal the back pain along with the traumas."

Two simple ways to forge a healthy connection with your survival speaker and the earth are 1) sit quietly outside on the earth using the Grounding Technique or 2) rest in the Child Pose yoga position.

2. Emotional Speaker

The emotional speaker is located directly below the navel and is associated with the gonads. This speaker has both a front and back. The front is where you express feelings, creativity and sexuality—it is also how you connect and respond emotionally toward others.

The back of this speaker involves emotional support issues.

Are you an empathetic listener? Do you take on the emotions and stress of others during conversations? When the front of this speaker is overly enlarged, you are led by your emotions. You overly concern yourself with others or overindulge in food or sex, whereas if you avoid emotional exchanges, the front of this speaker is partially blocked. You rely on logic to understand emotional situations.

Do you attract emotional support from others? Are you able to emotionally support yourself? If there are blocks in the back of the speaker, you won't attract emotional support from others and probably aren't supporting yourself emotionally. If the back of this speaker is enlarged, you may manipulate others emotionally to meet your needs.

This speaker is constantly dealing with intense emotions. Subsequently, it is easily overwhelmed, which causes confusion regarding whose feelings are whose. If you experience lower abdomen or reproductive issues, it's time to pay attention to emotional exchanges, patterns or empathetic habits along with the physical symptoms.

Grounding and balancing this speaker allows you to share emotionally with others in a balanced way, at the same time attracting the emotional support you need. Remember, emotions keep you real. They are a vital link between the body and mind, keeping all aspects of the self in balance.

3. Power Speaker

Power games are common in today's world. The first step in finding a solution to these conflicts is knowing where the interaction is taking place in your body. The next step is to disengage by setting healthy boundaries. The power speaker is located in the middle of your torso and associated with the pancreas. It involves the will and personal power.

Keep in mind that you cannot change the energy patterns of others, but you can change your own. Whether you are the sender or receiver in a power trip, becoming aware of how you use your energy identifies your role as either aggressor or victim.

Like the emotional speaker, the power speaker has a front and back. If you rely on your will to control others, the front of the power speaker is enlarged. Whereas, if you subordinate your will to the desires of others, the front is weak or contracted.

If the back of this speaker is partially closed, you won't feel powerful in your own right. You may, as a result, unconsciously misuse your power in an attempt to control others. If the back is enlarged, you manipulate others in an attempt to feel superior or to achieve your goals.

If your stomach is in knots most of the time or you notice others clutching their stomach when they are around you, it's time to ground and balance your power speaker. When you are secure in yourself, using your personal power wisely in daily interactions, you then empower others instead of engaging in petty power trips.

4. Heart Speaker

The phrase "come from your heart" may not seem relevant in today's aggressive and competitive world, but it can work effectively and ethically for everyone. The heart speaker is the doorway to your inner core. Consequently, speaking from your heart is a powerful way to communicate since your inner instincts and senses are engaged.

Located in the middle of your chest and associated with the thymus gland, the heart speaker is where you give and receive love and express your personal truth. Additionally, it is the place where you connect with compassion, universal understanding and unity.

Like the emotional and power speakers, the heart speaker also has a front and back. When the front of this speaker is partly contracted or blocked, you have a hard time expressing your personal truth, compassion or love. If this speaker is enlarged, you are able to express love but are not comfortable on the receiving end.

If the back is blocked or contracted, you may attract painful experiences, feel victimized or betrayed by others. If the back is enlarged, you tend to manipulate others to feel loved. If you've ever felt like someone stabbed you in the back, this description is an accurate account of what happens to you on an energy level. Feelings of betrayal, if not resolved, continue to attract similar situations until the issue is healed.

Speaking from your core through your heart center allows you to be clearly heard and understood. Since the heart speaker is where you express your personal truth, it is critical to keep this energy center clear and balanced. When you speak from your core, you also engage the other person's core, whether they realize it or not. In essence, you are communicating from your best self while calling on their best self. You'll find that conversations improve and reflect this connection.

Pain, stress or trauma associated with the heart and lung areas may be a reminder to take a closer look at how you give and receive love in your life. Grounding and balancing the heart speaker helps you express love and acceptance toward others. As you release old hurts and become true to yourself, you attract healthy and loving relationships that are more fulfilling.

5. Throat Speaker

Communication plays an increasingly important role in today's world. A fair amount of these interactions take place either over the phone, texting or the internet. Since these encounters are not always face-to-face, selecting your words carefully is of vital importance. Your tone and intent also play a role. The old saying "actions speak louder than words" does not apply in many situations, since the interactions are not in person. Miscommunication occurs more frequently when you can't see the person you're conversing with.

The throat speaker is located at the neck and is associated with the thyroid. This speaker has a front and back and governs speaking, listening, writing, drawing and musical expression. In addition to all forms of communication, this speaker involves dealing honestly with yourself and others.

If the front of this speaker is enlarged, you tend to interrupt during conversations, not allowing others to fully express themselves. However, if you agree with other people most of the time and don't express your view, the front is most likely weak or contracted.

The back of this speaker involves listening and honesty. Are you a good listener but don't communicate well? If so, the back of this speaker is enlarged. Do you tend to gossip? Are your dealings with others misleading or unclear? Chances are the back is blocked.

Grounding and balancing the throat speaker improves communition on all levels, promoting clear expression and thoughtful listening.

Last summer, I injured my neck while carrying a raft. It took six months to heal. Chiropractic treatments, physical therapy and massage were major components of my healing. Throughout this process were lessons. I had opportunities to work on attentive listening, speaking up for myself, choosing words carefully and watching my tone and intent. This injury allowed me to expand my body awareness, improve communication skills and have a deeper understanding and compassion for others with similar injuries.

6. Mental Speaker

In our mentally-focused society, headaches, migraines, insomnia and excessive mental chatter are common complaints. Although mental and visual stimulation involving television, the internet and video games is highly entertaining, it overtaxes the mind.

The mental speaker, located in the middle of the forehead, has a front and back and is associated with the pituitary gland. Imagination, insight and perception are are associated with the front of this speaker. Also related is the ability to focus and visualize ideas and goals. The back of this speaker involves the implementation of these goals and ideas, along with attention to detail.

Too much mental strain affects these areas and stifles your ability to move forward in life. If you visualize your goals but are unable to achieve them, chances are the front of this speaker is open and clear, and the back is blocked.

Subsequently, if you attend to all the details in life but have trouble formulating and implementing ideas and goals, the front of your speaker is blocked and the back is balanced.

Grounding and balancing the mental speaker improves focus and attention span, at the same time helping you manifest your goals and expand your vision.

7. Crown Speaker

Have you ever wondered if there is more to life than surviving the work week? Most of us set our sights on weekends and vacations as a reward for enduring the daily grind. Since the majority of our time is spent working, what we do for a living should be rewarding and fulfilling.

The crown speaker involves your purpose, potential and spirituality. It is located on top of the head and associated with the pineal gland. The crown speaker faces the universe and is the connection to universal energy. This important energy fuels your body and allows your psyche to let go on the physical, emotional and mental level.

If you were brought up with strict beliefs, have a need for control or deal with excessive guilt, your crown speaker has constricted or blocked areas. Similarly, if you continually strive to achieve certain goals only to find them unfulfilling, you probably have a blocked or unbalanced speaker.

A grounded and balanced crown speaker puts you in touch with your goals, purpose and highest potential! Additionally, it promotes adaptability and tolerance, providing a clear connection with your own spirituality.

8. & 9. Earth & Potential Speakers

Beside the seven major speakers located in the body, you also have two additional speakers, one above and one below. Together, these two speakers provide a solid base and structure for you.

The earth speaker is located two feet below your body in the ground. The potential speaker is located two feet above your head.

Think of the earth speaker as an important link between your physical body and the earth, giving the psyche a solid base or structure. Survival issues are healed by connecting your survival speaker to your earth speaker, helping your body connect to its roots.

The potential speaker contains pertinent information relating to your higher knowledge and wisdom. A strong connection between the crown speaker and potential speaker gives direct access to the highest insight and spirituality. **These two speakers align with your body and together make up your core structure.**

A Road Map of Your Body

9. Wisdom-Higher Knowledge

7. Inspiration-Spirituality-Flow

6. Goals-Direction

5. Communication

4. Personal Truth-Love

3. Personal Power

2. Emotional Expression

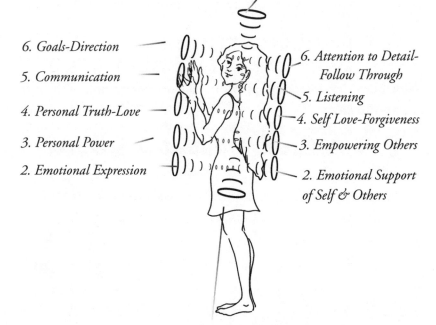

6. Attention to Detail-Follow Through

5. Listening

4. Self Love-Forgiveness

3. Empowering Others

2. Emotional Support of Self & Others

1. Grounding-Security-Trust

8. Earth Connection

A chiropractor has this to say about speaker awareness: "I know that healing involves body, mind and spirit. In case after case, the correlation of emotions to physical symptoms is very apparent. Throughout the day, my knowledge of the energy centers and my intuition spur me on to ask my patients the right questions that will lead to their healing solution."

The following techniques are designed to explore, ground and balance the seven major speakers in your body.

The Speaker Awareness Technique explores each speaker using your inner core. It combines touch, association and insight. Since some speakers have a front and back and others don't, the following information is useful.

Start with 1st speaker (see diagram on page 90). If you are male, this speaker is located at the base of your spine. If you are female, it is between your ovaries. To explore this speaker, place one hand on each side of your hips. Speakers 2-6 have a front and back. Placing one hand on the front of a specific speaker allows you to assess both front and back. Since the 7th speaker is located on the top of your head, simply place one hand there. As you explore a specific speaker, make sure to say its name out loud. The combination of touch and expression creates a strong association for the speaker. I find it helpful to use more than one modality when learning something new.

As you close your eyes and focus on each speaker, your instincts and insight engage. Since everyone receives their insight in different ways, make sure to pay attention to any thought, feeling, sense, picture or word that surfaces. Express the information out loud to start the flow of intuition. Since your insight is a new language, allow yourself to be led by your inner core.

Another method, the Speaker Technique, is a quick and efficient way to clear and balance each energy center using your fingers, core energy and the power of intention. This method utilizes nerve endings and meridians (energy channels) located in the fingers, along with the power of intention. It is great way of balancing on the go.

Speaker Awareness Technique

Key Phrase: "Center-Core-Ground-Balance"

~Sit or lie somewhere quiet and close your eyes. Shift your focus from head to heart by placing one hand on the middle of your chest. Focus there and say, **"Center- Core,"** out loud slowly.

~Start with the 1st or survival speaker. Place both hands on your hips. If you are male, focus at the base of your spine. If you are female, focus between your ovaries.

~Close your eyes and visualize your 1st-survival speaker as a small cone. If you can't see it, feel it or sense it, imagine it. Sense how this area feels. Is it tight, blocked or constricted? Is it calm and flowing? Is there a color to it?

~Now, say your key word, **"Ground,"** out loud from your heart. Note any changes. If this area feels fine, move your focus to the next speaker. However, if this area feels unbalanced, say the key word, **"Balance."** Take a few moments after each word to allow the intentions to work. If a speaker feels tense or anxious, calm it by saying, **"Orange."**

~The next five speakers have a front and back. Place one hand on the front of a specific speaker, taking a few moments to sense the energy of the area, using your key words if needed. Repeat this process for each speaker. Since the 7th or crown speaker is located on top of your head, place one hand there to assess this speaker.

Once you are familiar with all seven speakers, take a few moments during the day to check them. Use the following technique to balance them quickly, efficiently and independently. This method connects each speaker to a specific finger.

Speaker Technique

~Place one hand on your heart center and say, **"Center- Core,"** out loud slowly from there. This engages your core structure. Place your hands on your lap, palms facing the ceiling. Say your key word, **"Connect."** Wait until you sense an energy connection on your hands.

~Your right hand corresponds to the first five speakers. The thumb represents the 1st-survival speaker, the pointer finger signifies the 2nd-emotional speaker, the middle finger refers to the 3rd-power speaker, the ring finger relates to the 4th-heart speaker, and the small finger signifies the 5th-throat speaker. The thumb of the left hand represents the 6th-mental speaker, and the pointer finger, the 7th-crown speaker.

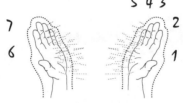

~When one or more speakers need grounding and balancing, use the corresponding fingers to clear them. Place the tip of the corresponding finger between your thumb and index finger, pressing firmly for about 15 seconds. Move the finger rapidly back and forth for 15 seconds. A calm energy will spread throughout the corresponding area. Repeat this process as needed.

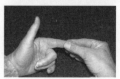

Quick reference: For fear or security issues, balance the 1st-survival speaker. For emotional issues or an upset stomach, ground the 2nd-emotional speaker. For more information, refer to the speaker section.

Now that you have

a road map of your body...

Explore your

personal space

Chapter 10

Personal Space

So sometimes all our identities become pushed
into the background as we take in bad energy or maybe as we,
I don't know, grow up and get a job or something...
　　　　　　　　　　　　　　　　　　　　—Ani Difranco

The world is rapidly changing, becoming more complex and crowded. Each day we are constantly surrounded with the hustle and bustle of people, traffic, noise and deadlines.

Finding ways to cope with so much stimuli is essential for your well-being. One way to do this is by creating a healthy personal space around the physical body. Personal space acts as a buffer zone between your body and the busy world you live in.

This space already exists and is known as the energy field; it expresses who you are and what you are feeling at any given moment. Whether or not it is healthy is another matter. As you encounter constant stress and frenetic energy throughout the day, your personal space fills up with your own stress, along with the energy of people you encounter and the places you inhabit.

Chronic stress or pain adversely affects your energy field by wearing down your natural boundary, thereby reducing the energy flow in and around the body.

A healthy energy field is made up of three feet of personal space and is divided into five levels. Comprehending these levels increases your awareness, promoting healthy communication and balance between the body, emotions and intellect.

Personal Space Diagram

1. Physical Level: This level consists of energy within the physical body. Clear this level daily to increase the energy flow and release blocked energy within the body.

2. Etheric Level: The etheric level is a magnetic field that surrounds the physical body. This level is a healthy barrier between the emotions and body. Trauma, stress, pain, smoking, alcohol and drugs weaken this field. Clear and renew this level daily to keep a healthy buffer between the emotions and body.

3. Emotional Level: This level houses our ever changing emotions and is the link between mind and body communication. Clear this level daily to prevent depression and ensure emotional well-being.

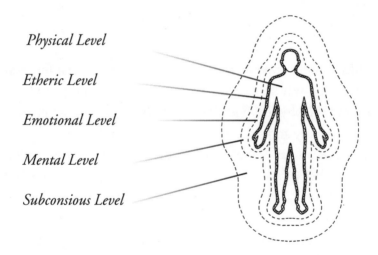

Physical Level

Etheric Level

Emotional Level

Mental Level

Subconsious Level

4. Mental Level: This level relates to logic and mental expression. Clear this level daily to release mental fatigue and prevent insomnia.

5. Subconsious Level: This level houses our subconscious patterns and projections along with the collected stress from our daily encounters. Cleanse this level daily to provide a clear expression of yourself and a more accurate view of the world around you.

The Physical Level

Energy within the body makes up the physical level. If you are active and in touch with your body, the energy within feels light and fluid. However, if your body has experienced trauma or is in chronic pain, stress or anxiety, it feels dense and heavy. Areas that hold blocked energy for a prolonged amount of time separate from the energy flow of the body, trapping pain and stress and are more susceptible to illness.

The Etheric Level

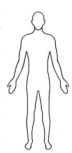

The level closest to the physical body is called the etheric level. Derived from the word *ether*, it is the state between energy and matter. This level consists of a net-like covering that surrounds the physical body. Also known as the magnetic field, it extends one to two inches beyond your body. This level is a natural protection which acts as a buffer between the emotions and body.

When someone is missing a limb or another part of their body, the etheric level still holds the basic shape of the missing part. This explains why people continue to feel sensations associated with missing body parts.

Intense trauma weakens the etheric level, as do cigarettes, alcohol or drugs. The latter create artificial barriers that are a temporary fix, although habitual use adversely affects this level.

If the emotional level continuously impinges on your physical body, the resulting stress may cause numerous physical problems such as hypersensitivity, nervousness, anxiety or fibromyalgia. Take a few moments to ground, clear and strengthen this level regularly. This ensures a healthy buffer between your body and emotions which prevents depression and disease.

The Emotional Level

The emotional level, third level in your personal space, continuously expresses and radiates feelings and emotions for better or worse. This level extends eight to ten inches beyond the body—depending on how full it is. If you feel depressed much of the time, your emotional level is overflowing and pressing against the etheric field, creating a feeling of depression. Empty this level on a regular basis, just as you would an overflowing vacuum bag or garbage can. Clearing your personal space makes a huge difference in the way you operate and feel.

If you are a predominantly logic-based person, you tend to avoid emotions. Most likely you rely on reason and detachment when dealing with emotional situations. Unfortunately, avoidance of your emotional state works only for so long. A build-up of repressed emotions eventually leads to depression. Antidepressants may work well for you as a short-term solution, since you are used to avoiding how you feel. Although you may not experience the effects of depression because of the medication, the repressed emotions continue to build.

On the other hand, if you are an emotionally-based person, you understand the world though feelings—your own and others'. Therefore, since you feel emotions more strongly, you are more prone to depression. Antidepressants tend to buffer you from your feelings. Since you are less comfortable relying on logic, these drugs may leave you feeling lost and disconnected from your primary function, your emotions.

Remember, emotions are your psyche's way of saying "that's enough" when your mind wants to keep going and find ways to cope. A great way to have emotional clarity is to ground and clear this level daily. The payoff is less emotional baggage to weigh you down and you gain a quick, easy way to balance your emotions and intellect.

The Mental Level

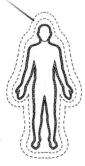

The mental level, fourth level in your personal space, involves logic, linear thinking and mental expression. This level extends eight to ten inches beyond the emotional level. With the onset of television and computers, overusing the mental capacity has become the norm. As you become mentally-driven, you detach, resulting in a loss of awareness of your physical and emotional needs.

This is also true when coping with chronic pain. To avoid discomfort in the body, both the intellect and will take over and pain is isolated or ignored. This approach takes a toll on the emotional state and decreases body awareness. A mentally-based person may not feel physical symptoms since they tend to avoid emotions, the bridge between the mind and body. They may have a sudden onset of illness without experiencing the warning signs or symptoms. However, an emotionally-based person will feel warning signs and symptoms, although they may overreact or exaggerate the symptoms without the balance of the mental level.

Whether you experience chronic stress or pain or your thoughts tend to race out of control, taking a few moments to ground and clear this level will bring instant relief. Since too much mental strain causes headaches and insomnia, shifting your focus from head to heart gives the mental level a much needed break.

Clearing this level on a daily basis positively affects your mental health. With a clear mental level, you focus on what is most important on your day's agenda, expressing your ideas in a more organized and creative manner.

The Subconscious Level

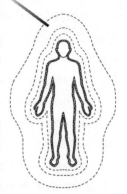

The subconscious level is the fifth level surrounding the body. It extends approximately a foot and a half beyond the mental level. This level contains your unowned emotions and patterns, and the collected stress of the day.

This level is wild and untamed and does not respond well to control. Just when you think you're on track in life, your subconscious steps in and disrupts your well-laid plans, sabotaging your goals and happiness. At other times, it leads you to healthier relationships, a deeper understanding of yourself or new beginnings. Grounding and clearing this level neutralizes emotions or patterns likely to sabotage your goals and happiness. When this level is clear, you have a better understanding of both your conscious and subconscious parts, thereby projecting a lucid reflection of who you are. Moreover, clearing the subconscious level before sleep helps you remember your dreams, allowing an easier transition to wakefulness with more clarity.

In the words of a front office receptionist, "I am the first friendly face that people see as they walk in the door. The constant bombardment of answering phones and greeting the public is mentally and emotionally wearing. When I feel I am at my wits' end, I clear both my personal space and my work space, immediately feeling the change in myself and in the office."

Clear your personal space first thing in the morning, during the day and before bedtime. Notice the difference in the way you carry yourself and how others respond to you. Clear all five levels together or each level individually when you have time. Taking the time to clear your space regularly allows your body to find its balance and return to its natural state of being.

Personal Space Exercise

Key Words: "Center-Core-Connect-Let go"
Remember to allow this technique to happen rather than forcing it.

~Shift your focus from head to heart by placing your hand on the middle of your chest. Say, **"Center-Core,"** out loud from your heart. This engages your core structure.

~Raise your hands over your head with palms facing toward the ceiling. Say, **"Connect,"** out loud from your heart. When you feel core energy in the palm of your hands, you are ready to proceed.

~Say, **"Let go,"** out loud from your heart. Allow your inner core energy to guide your hands. As your arms start to move on their own, they will attract any stuck energy in your personal space.

~As your hands reach your sides, take a moment to shake off any stuck energy still clinging to them. If your personal space still feels heavy, repeat this exercise again.

~If time or space is limited, complete this exercise without the arm movements.

Note: Clear all five levels at once or each level individually. To clear a specific level, start the technique by saying the specific level. For example, say, **"Physical Level"** or "Level 1," followed by your key words, **"Center-Core-Connect-Let go."**

Now that you have an

understanding of your

personal space...

Expand your intuition

Chapter 11

Intuition

Often you just have to rely on your intuition.
—Bill Gates

We live in a multidimensional universe unlimited by time and space. Immersed in today's fast-paced technological world, we tend to lose sight of the wonders surrounding us on all levels. With the stream of information flowing past our consciousness from every direction, it is increasingly difficult to make sense of the chaos we encounter daily. **However, you can make the decision to look within, accessing what is available at your core—your intuition.** Looking inward, you tap into your insight—the part that sees endless possibilities and knows no limits.

Throughout evolution, humankind has depended on intuition for survival, self awareness and new discoveries. Early humans used this insight to align themselves with the cycles of nature and the flow of life, since their survival depended on it. Down through history, world leaders, prophets, philosophers and scientists also trusted their intuition to guide them. Today, after centuries of relying on rational thinking, cultures around the world are experiencing a resurgence of interest in the intuitive realm. Intuition is increasingly emerging as a necessary tool for meeting the constant challenges of life.

There is a potential inside you that knows your true self and understands your deepest desires. **It has the ability to access information unavailable to your outer senses. It offers a new language—in a sense, a new intelligence.** The term *intuition* means attaining direct knowledge without using rational thought. It is used

103

to describe a wide variety of inner abilities. We all possess these abilities, whether we acknowledge them or not. Women talk about their intuition; men simply follow their hunches or gut. As you actively develop your inner senses, it's time to consciously integrate them into your daily life. When crises arise, you can access your insight, which guides you to the right solutions.

Although your five outer senses guide you every day, you also use your corresponding inner senses. You may call them hunches, feelings, insight, flashes of intuition or senses. Regardless of what you call them, the key is to pay attention to them. Shifting your focus from head to heart and engaging your core makes you more conscious of them, increasing your awareness. The next step is to connect directly with your intuition while giving it a secure base.

Most of us have experienced a time when we were in touch with our intuition. A strong feeling or gut reaction took hold deep within; we knew just how to act—when to take that chance. This knowingness tends to arise in times of crisis or when we are at crossroads in life. Why wait for a crisis to experience your intuition?

Since intuition is a blend of thoughts, feelings, words, pictures and senses, it is helpful to create a structure when first attempting to access it. You accomplish this by enlisting the help of your left and right brain. Since the left brain responds well to structure and likes to control situations, it is used to set up a workable base and strategy for your insight. The simple steps of shifting your focus to your heart and engaging your core keeps your left brain occupied. This allows the more free flowing part of your psyche, your right brain, to access the multi-dimensional language of your subconscious self.

Wiring your intuition directly establishes a circuitry that allows you to access your intuition anytime. For this connection, you need to utilize two speakers, the 8th-earth speaker, located two feet below you in the earth and the 9th-potential speaker, located two feet above your head. Think of your earth speaker as an important link between your physical body and the earth. The potential speaker contains pertinent information relating to your higher goals, knowledge and purpose. Connecting with these two speakers allows you to access information from your intuition while giving it a secure base, enabling you to use the information in a practical way.

A simple way to bypass the easily distracted conscious mind is to wire the earth and potential speakers directly to your hands. Once the wiring is in place, all that is needed is to engage your inner core to guide your hands. Allowing your core to guide your hands is a powerful means of letting go. It is also a direct and safe way to tune into your intuition.

Learning this new way of accessing your insight takes some practice and trust. To succeed, at first you need patience and a willingness to be unconcerned whether the information you receive is right or wrong. Tapping into your intuition is like learning a new language. Each step of the way, it is important to ask questions and interpret the answers you receive. However, despite the challenges, this new relationship is one of the most important you make, since it involves a conscious decision to connect to the clear, knowing part of you.

The Balancing Technique involves a two-handed method directly connecting you to your intuition and is similar to kinesiology or muscle testing. As it grounds both connections to the earth, this enables any changes to manifest quickly in the physical world. This method also helps you interpret the situation while allowing your inner core to clear any resistance or blocks energetically. Since everything in life is made of energy—clearing blocks, patterns or issues energetically is the quickest way to achieve success. It is simple, effective and does not require much practice.

We all have aspects of our psyche that sabotage our progress and don't align with our goals. Since these patterns, issues or blocked energies reside in the subconscious, you're probably unaware of their agendas. However, they hinder your progress and keep you unfocused.

This technique allows you to access these subconscious parts and align them with your goals.

Select an aspect in your life that needs integrating or balancing. It may be a goal you want to achieve, a relationship that needs attention, a pattern you need to release or a physical, emotional or mental concern that needs healing. Since the balancing takes place energetically between your hands, it enables you to detach mentally and emotionally from whatever is impeding your progress. With the help of your insight and inner core, you transform blocked energy into flowing energy to release a pattern or heal an issue. Since energy is the fastest way to achieve balance and healing, progress manifests and integrates more quickly. If the situation involves a long-standing pattern or issue, you may need to repeat this process daily until the energy feels balanced.

This method also releases stress and pain. When the physical body experiences chronic distress, it becomes isolated and separate from the rest of the body. The longer this continues, the more separate these parts become. Consequently, they don't respond to the usual treatments that offer relief. This technique reaches these isolated parts with help from the inner core and initiates the healing. You may notice physical symptoms disappear as you use this tool.

Balancing Technique

Key Phrase: "Center-Core-Connect-Activate-(Intention)"

~Place one hand on the middle of your chest. Say, **"Center-Core,"** out loud from your heart center. This engages your core structure.

~Place your hands on your lap, palms facing the ceiling. Say, **"Connect,"** from your heart. When you sense an energy connection on your hands, you are ready.

~Choose an aspect of your life that needs attention—attaining a goal, balancing a relationship, releasing a pattern or healing a mental, emotional or physical concern.

~Hold your hands 8 to 10 inches apart facing each other. Select one hand to represent a goal, pattern, issue or concern. The other hand signifies your core. For situations involving relationships, one hand represents the person and the opposite hand represents you.

New Job   *Your Core*

~Next, assess the situation energetically, by saying, **"Activate."** Sense the energy in front of each hand. Does it feel imbalanced or blocked? Which hand is it? The one representing you? Another person? The situation? Both hands? This provides insight into the situation.

~Create a new structure based on trust. Say the key word, **"Trust."** Clear the pathway energetically by choosing an intention and saying it from your heart. Some examples are, **"Integrate, Balance, Heal, Manifest, Openness, Communication, Transform, Release, Neutralize, Best possible outcome, Empower."** Once the situation is energetically balanced, the change quickly manifests in the physical world.

The Intuition Technique is a more specific tool—allowing you to communicate directly with your inner core by structuring your insight with yes-no signals. When first consciously attempting to use intuition, you may experience a mental struggle. Much of this resistance comes from the intellect. As your mind strives for control, it blocks your inner voice. Shifting your focus from head to heart solves this dilemma. Your mind can continue its antics, since your focus is elsewhere and can't be distracted.

An engineer and co-founder of a biochemical firm explains: "I am sometimes involved in numerous presentations and tend to be very mental. During group interactions my ego gets in the way. Taking the time to ground, center and come from my heart keeps my ego in check and allows my intuitive part to take over. I am then able to read the group more effectively, understand their needs and reach them in a more balanced and successful manner."

This technique enables you to ask specific questions of your insight about situations, patterns, health issues or relationships. When first starting this process, an important point to remember is that anything you try on an inner level is accomplished by allowing, rather than pushing or controlling. As you take the first steps, you may wonder whether you are proceeding in the "right" way. Let go of this belief system and you will soon realize that you can learn as much from a "wrong" answer as a "right" one.

On a personal note, one day while waiting for my six-year-old daughter at our neighborhood bus stop, I panicked as the school bus pulled up, emptied out and I realized she wasn't on it. I immediately thought to myself, "Is she okay?" Before I could mentally think of an answer, my hand responded with a *yes* signal. My inner core answered my question. Intuitively aware that she was safe, I calmed down enough to retrace her steps and discovered she had gotten off the bus at my sister's house. That was the day my trust in my intuition could no longer be questioned.

Intuition Technique

~Shift your focus from head to heart by placing one hand on the middle of your chest. Say, **"Center-Core,"** out loud from your heart, engaging your core structure.

~Place both hands on your lap, palms up toward the ceiling. Say, **"Connect,"** out loud from your heart. This intention connects your intuition directly to your hands. When you sense an energy connection on your hands, you are connected.

~Select one hand to signify a *yes* answer—the opposite hand for *no.* Test your accuracy by asking three questions that you know the answers. For example: *Are my eyes blue? Do I have brown hair? Am I five feet tall?* Ask the questions out loud when possible, waiting for a strong energy response on the corresponding hand. Once you receive correct answers to the sample questions, you're ready to proceed.

One hand for *yes.*   One hand for *no.*

~Formulate your questions in a *yes-no* format, waiting for your intuition to respond with energy. If an answer is incorrect, don't worry. Shift your focus back to your heart center, repeat the steps and try again. Sometimes you receive *yes* and *no* sensations at the same time. This means you need to re-define your questions in a clearer format, or there is no clear answer at this time. Play with your *yes-no* method throughout your day, not judging whether it is right or wrong. As you learn to communicate with your inner core, you create a strong and lasting relationship with your insight, an invaluable tool for life.

Now that you have

consciously engaged

your intuition...

Explore your

elements and functions

Chapter 12

The Elements & Functions

The mind, intellect, ego, ether, air, fire, water and earth are the eightfold transformation of My nature.
—Bhagavad Gita

Ask someone you know to describe their own personality. The description you receive from them probably differs greatly from that of their relatives, friends or co-workers. Most people's view of themselves is incomplete, since it's seen through the filter of their ego and limited belief system. The less desirable qualities are often hidden within the subconscious self. Similarly, most of us are comfortable developing our strengths and natural abilities while ignoring our weaker abilities. Recognizing and understanding the less desirable parts of our personalities help us attain a more balanced sense of self and a clearer picture of our true nature. Thus, working on the weaker abilities opens up new avenues and opportunities for growth.

The four functions, as categorized in Carl Jung's psychological types, are an easy way to develop a deeper understanding of the way we perceive ourselves and others. These functions involve thinking, intuition, sensing and feeling, corresponding to the four elements of air, fire, earth and water.

Ether, the fifth element, because of its integrative properties, is used here in conjunction with inner core energy. Together, they infuse and integrate the above elements and functions.

We all use these four functions in varying degrees to perceive our world. **Each function and element have distinct characteristics and tendencies and govern specific systems and organs in the body.**

The thinking-air function corresponds to predominantly intellectual people who are rational, reasonable, full of ideas and able to communicate well. However, when it comes to feelings, this type of person can seem distant, aloof or noncommittal. These individuals state their opinion by using the words, *I think...* Circulation, heart and lungs are the physical components associated with air.

Intuition-fire function individuals are described as outgoing, action-oriented, quick, intuitive and visionary. They are sometimes flighty, impulsive and tactless. A typical response for this type of person is, *Why should I explain, I just know.* Fire rules digestion, stomach and vitality.

The sensing-earth function relates to people who perceive life through the five senses. These people are practical, efficient, artistic or musical and have an understanding of the material world. They can also be apprehensive, narrow-minded and selfish. If something isn't tangible, this type of person has a difficult time relating to it. *I don't see your point, since I haven't experienced it...*is a common response of someone with this primary function. Earth governs the elimination of solids and liquids, the bladder and rectum.

The feeling-water function describes deeply emotional people who are loving, giving, caring, compassionate and empathetic. They may also be moody, possessive and lacking in boundaries. When asked their opinion about a situation, this type of person respond with, *I feel...* Physically speaking, water rules the reproductive organs, glands and emotional drive.

Everyone has different combinations of primary and secondary functions which are uniquely theirs. Becoming familiar and actively developing your secondary processes as well as primary ones, leads to a broader understanding of your true nature.

Element Imbalances

The stress, pain and trauma of daily events takes its toll on your body, resulting in an excess or lack of elements within your system.

Too much air manifests in overthinking, mental chatter, unhealthy detachment or a compelling need to "get things done." A lack of air manifests as stagnation, mental patterns, criticalness or a need for control. Physical symptoms or ailments are sinus or throat problems, psoriasis, headaches, asthma, emphysema or heart arrhythmia.

An excess of fire results in too much adrenaline pulsing through the body, an inability to turn off at night, frequent episodes of burnout, uncontrolled anger and depleted energy resources. A lack of fire manifests as quick, ambitious starts that lack follow-through, inertia, resentment, blame or jealousy. Physical manifestations are arthritis, nervousness, tension, heart issues, hardening of arteries or hot flashes.

An overabundance of earth manifests as weight gain, sluggishness, density or building up walls. Not enough earth manifests as an inability to meet basic needs, lack of focus, spacey feelings or low self-esteem. Physical issues involve gastric ulcers, overeating or poor appetite, nausea or digestive tract problems.

An excess of water floods the system, causing exaggerated emotional responses, depression, extreme moodiness or smothering tendencies. Insufficient water results in obsession, isolation, neediness or dependency. Physical symptoms include water weight, bladder issues, dehydration, sciatica or joint issues.

"I am someone who processes primarily through feeling and intuition. Over time, I have come to realize that I need to cultivate my intellect and sensing functions to better achieve my goals. I use teaching, writing and making lists to work on my air-thinking function. Activities such as gardening and running have a grounding effect and help me develop my instinctual nature. As I tend to live an active life, I find that making time in my busy schedule to relax and reflect, balances me and prevents emotional and physical burnout."

Over the years, I have encountered clients whose natural tendencies or primary functions were interrupted in their early years. Traumatic or intense experiences cause this type of disconnect, forcing the person to unconsciously align with a function they have no natural affinity for. When this occurs, life seems especially difficult for them.

On sharing this insight with clients, a look of deep relief spreads across their faces, along with a desire to explore this new information. Although this is not a common occurrence, it is something to keep in mind when exploring your own functions.

Imagine a young child with a sensitive emotional and sensing nature raised in an extremely turbulent household. The constant fighting and dysfunction overwhelm his sensitive nature, causing him to detach and rely on intellect to survive the turmoil. Growing up, he intuitively learns to placate others to avoid conflicts, at the same time ignoring his own emotional needs. As an adult, he avoids emotional outbursts at all costs, but inside still craves the emotional closeness of his true nature. Although he is competent at using his intellect, he never quite feels at home in this function. Luckily, he finds that outdoor activities such as hiking, camping, fishing and biking give him stability and peace as only nature can.

Elements and Inner Senses

The four functions also house inner abilities. Recognizing and developing these insights add a whole new dimension to your world.

1. Air-Thinking Function
INNER SENSES
Perception-Clairvoyance-Pictures

2. Fire-Intuitive Function
INNER SENSES
Flash-Insight-Knowingness

3. Earth-Sensing Function
INNER SENSES
Clairaudience-Sensing-Psychometry

4. Water-Feeling Function
INNER SENSES
Clairsentience-Empathy

For definitions of inner senses, see the Glossary on page 136.

The Four Functions Technique uses your insight to assess your primary and secondary functions. The results may confirm what you already know about yourself or surprise you by uncovering primary functions interrupted in childhood.

The Healing Hands Technique offers a quick, easy method to balance and integrate all four functions and elements, along with your inner and outer instincts and senses. One hand represents your subconscious nature, the other hand your conscious nature. The fingers correspond to the functions and elements. This method makes use of nerve endings and meridians located in the fingertips, along with the power of intention. The integration of inner core energy and ether infuses all components, initiating the move toward higher consciousness and wisdom. You may experience relief of physical symptoms as you balance and ground each element and its corresponding functions and physicalities. This method is simple and is effective for problems like overthinking, running on adrenaline, chronic pain or stress, feelings of burnout or lack of focus. Try it anytime there are a few free moments or a lull in activities.

Four Functions Technique

Key Words: "Center-Core-Connect"
Remember to allow this technique to happen rather than forcing it.

~Use this technique to identify your primary and secondary functions. Use the thumb and next three fingers on your right hand to represent the four functions. The thumb signifies the thinking-air function, the pointer finger corresponds to the intuition-fire function, the middle finger relates to the sensing-earth function and the ring finger represents the feeling-water function.

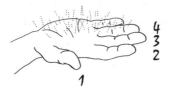

~Place one hand at your heart center and say the key words, "**Center-Core,**" out loud slowly from there. Next, place your hands on your lap and say the key word, "**Connect.**" This wires your 8th and 9th speakers directly to your hands. When you sense an energy connection on your palms, state the following, "**Show me my primary functions.**" Focus at your heart center, waiting quietly for a response. If you don't receive a clear response, go through the steps again, making sure to allow your fingers to respond while staying out of your head. Once you receive a clear response, say, "**Show me my secondary functions.**"

~Note whether finger responses match your conscious conclusions. Take some time to reflect on some new activities you can try to expand your secondary functions. In doing so, you balance all four functions, expanding your potential in all areas.

Try the following technique to integrate all functions, release and balance symptoms and elements, and infuse all areas with ether and inner core energy.

Healing Hands Technique

This technique provides a quick way to balance and integrate the different parts of your psyche. The thumb and first three fingers correspond to the four elements and their functions based on Carl Jung's four psychological types: thinking-air function, intuition-fire function, sensing-earth function and feeling-water function. The little finger signifies the integration of ether and inner core energy used to infuse both elements and functions.

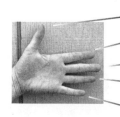
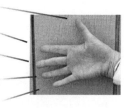

Thinking - Air Function
Intuition - Fire Function
Sensing - Earth Function
Feeling - Water Function
Integration - Ether - Core

~Your two hands respectively represent your conscious and subconscious parts of self. If you are right-handed, this hand represents your conscious self. Your left hand signifies your subconscious self. If you are a left-handed person, the opposite is true.

~Starting with the right hand, place the tip of your thumb between your opposite thumb and index finger, pressing firmly for 15 seconds. As you close your eyes and apply pressure to your  thumb, notice the corresponding body response. You may feel a tightness, sensitivity or pain. If so, wiggle the thumb for fifteen seconds to clear and balance this area. Then ground this area by holding the thumb firmly for the same amount of time. Continue until the area feels calm. Repeat the process with the opposite thumb.

~Continue with each finger, paying attention to your body responses. This technique releases trapped pain and stress throughout the body and integrates the elements and functions, infusing them with ether and inner core energy.

Put it all together,

integrating these techniques

into your life...

Introducing

daily survival skills

Chapter 13

Daily Survival Skills

The survival of the fittest is the ageless law of nature,
but the fittest are rarely strong.
The fittest are those endowed with the qualifications
for adaptation, the ability to accept the inevitable
and conform to the unavoidable, to harmonize with
existing or changing conditions.

—Unknown

Now that you've been introduced to a variety of survival skills throughout these chapters, it's time to integrate these techniques into your day in a simple and practical way.

Shift from a mental focus to a whole body awareness. This gives your mind a break, allowing you to experience the perfect moment and see the world with expanded vision and insight.

Ground your body with the earth to feel supported, connected and to heighten your awareness of your body's needs. Connect with the universal flow to inspire, create, let go and increase your energy flow.

Choose the path of strength to align with life's flow, attract what you need and allow your inner core to lead.

Clear your personal space in the morning to express yourself clearly and increase your understanding of others.

Speak from your core throughout the day, your place of honesty and personal truth. This improves communication and promotes the best in others.

Create healthy boundaries and reaction time by using the "Talk to the hand" Technique in person and on the phone.

When distress strikes, use the Manual Grounding Technique to release the "fight or flight" response. Next, use the Pain & Stress

Technique to send any distress into the ground.

Balance and integrate your primary and secondary functions quickly and efficiently by using the Healing Hands Technique.

To transition from a stressful day to a restful night, use the Manual Grounding Technique.

Clear your space at night to help you remember your dreams and provide an easier transition to wakefulness with more clarity.

An accounting manager states: "There are lots of methods for relieving pain and stress in our lives. Transcendental meditation works for many. Others prefer yoga, psychiatric therapy or pharmaceuticals. The methods in this book work for me. The simple principles of becoming centered on one's core energy, being grounded in trust and connected to the universal flow of life are concepts I relate to. They not only give me that short-term drug-like fix, but also the foundation for long-term health maintenance—both physical and mental."

What follows is a quick and easy guide to help reset your body to its natural state and energy flow. Use this guide any time you are knocked off balance by the distress of the day. These techniques promote adaptability, acceptance of present circumstances and the ability to "go with the flow" in ever changing conditions.

Daily Survival Skills

In the Morning...

~ Grounding Technique
Give your body a secure base and increase your energy flow

~ Personal Space Technique
Release stress, mental strain and depression in your space

During the Day...

~ Speak from Your Core
Place one hand at your heart center and speak from there

~ "Talk to the Hand" Technique
Deflect others' stress in person and on the phone

~ Boundary Technique
Renew your boundary when needed

~ Personal Space Technique
Clear your space as needed

When Stress or Pain Strikes...

~ Manual Grounding Technique
Use when stress or pain strikes and before bedtime

~ Balancing Technique
Use to access trapped pain or stress or to attract what you need

~ Pain Release Technique
Release pain or stress on specific areas in the body

~ Healing Hands Technique
Balance your speakers and functions

Grounding Technique

Key Phrase: "Center-Trust-Flow-Core-Ground"
Remember to allow this technique to happen rather than forcing it.

~Start the day with this exercise. Close your eyes and shift your focus by placing one hand at your heart center. Say, **"Center,"** out loud from there.

~Connect with the earth and universe and increase your energy flow by saying, **"Trust-Flow,"** slowly out loud from your heart center.

~Engage your inner core and say, **"Core,"** out loud from your heart. Take a deep breath and feel core energy surround you.

~Lay both hands on your lap, palms toward the ceiling and say, **"Ground."**

Quick Version: During the day, when life disrupts your grounding, engage your core and increase your energy flow with this method. Say the key words, **"Center-Core-Ground,"** out loud from your heart. Earth and universal energy automatically engage.

Ground your living space at the same time that you ground yourself. Simply expand your intention to include both.

Note: When you feel like your mind and will have taken over your day, plug into life's flow by closing your eyes, placing your hands on your lap palms up, and saying, **"Strength,"** out loud from your heart. Allow this energy to calm, revitalize and transform your day.

Personal Space Technique

Key Words: "Center-Core-Connect-Let go"

~Shift your focus from head to heart by placing your hand on the middle of your chest. Say, **"Center-Core,"** out loud from your heart. This engages your core structure.

~Raise your hands over your head with palms facing toward the ceiling. Say, **"Connect,"** out loud from your heart. Wait until you feel core energy in the palms of your hands. You are now ready to proceed.

~Say, **"Let go,"** out loud from your heart. Allow your inner core energy to guide your hands. As your arms start to move on their own, they will attract any stuck energy in your personal space.

~When your hands reach your sides, take a moment to shake any stuck energy still clinging to them. If your personal space still feels heavy, repeat this exercise again.

~If there is limited time or space, complete this exercise without the arm movements.

Note: Clear all five levels at once or each level individually. To clear a specific level, start the technique by saying the specific level. For example: say, **"Level 1"** or **"Physical Level,"** followed by your key words, **"Center-Core-Connect-Let go."**

Core-to-Core Communication

~During conversations, remember to speak from your inner core, your place of strength and personal truth. Not only do you present your best self, you engage the other person's core whether they realize it or not. Conversations improve and communication is more clear when you speak from your core.

"Talk to the Hand" Technique

~When the phone rings, raise your hand and allow whoever is on the other end to "talk to the hand." This deflects the other person's energy to your hand and gives your throat a needed break.

~During conversations, don't listen with your stomach. Instead, deflect their energy and have them "talk to the hand."

~If it is inconvenient to use your hand as a boundary, redirect the energy by imagining the other person's energy veering right or left as it meets your personal space. Place one hand on your knee to guide the energy past you while protecting your stomach area.

A magazine or note pad held up against your stomach can also be used as a quick boundary to deflect the energy of others. This redirection of energy gives your body a needed break—allowing you to enjoy the company of others, while not taking on their stress or pain.

Boundary Technique

Key Phrase: "Center-Core-Expand"

~Take a moment during the day to renew your boundary. Place one hand on the middle of your chest. Say, **"Center-Core,"** out loud slowly from there.

~Take a breath and as you breathe out, say, **"Expand,"** out loud from your heart center. Allow your core energy to surround you, renewing your boundaries.

Quick Version: Renew your boundary by saying, **"Center-Core-Expand,"** out loud from your heart. Take a breath and as you breathe out, your core energy sets a healthy boundary.

Computer Boundary Technique

Key Phrase: "Center-Core-Expand"

~As you turn on your computer, take a few moments to set a neutral boundary. Place your hand in front of the screen and feel the energy radiating from it. Keep your hand there as you follow the next step.

~Place your other hand in the middle of your chest and focus there. Say, **"Center-Core-Expand,"** out loud slowly from your heart.

~You'll feel core energy emanate from your hand. This energy creates a buffer between you and the computer. Renew this boundary hourly.

Manual Grounding Technique

Key Phrase: "Center-Trust-Flow-Core"

~Place one hand on your heart and say, **"Center,"** out loud from there.

~To increase the energy flow between your feet and your head, grasp the middle bottom of each foot or place tennis balls under both 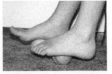 feet. Say the key word, **"Trust,"** out loud from your heart. Allow earth energy to calm and energize you for 30-60 seconds.

~Place one hand over your forehead (to calm the mental chatter) and the other hand the base of your skull (your  "fight or flight" area). Say, **"Flow,"** out loud from your heart center. Allow universal energy to calm and release any stress or pain in your head.

~To balance the left and right sides of the body, gently grasp the top of both ears and pull up firmly for 30 seconds to one minute (Photo A).

 A.    B.    C.

Gently pull on the bottom of both ear lobes for the same amount of time (Photo B). Pull out on the middle edge of both ears (Photo C).

~Find two areas on your upper chest that are tender (see picture for placement). Say, **"Core,"** out loud from  your heart and wiggle your fingers gently for 15 seconds. Then hold your fingers still for the same amount of time. Repeat until soreness is gone.

Pain Release Technique

Key Phrase: "Center-Core-Forward-Orange-Release"

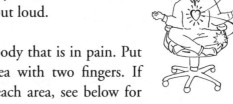

~Move your focus from head to heart by placing one hand on the middle of your chest. Focus there and say, **"Center- Core,"** out loud.

~Choose an area of your body that is in pain. Put slight pressure on this area with two fingers. If the pain is in a hard-to-reach area, see below for instructions.

~Say the key word, **"Forward."** This releases the band of will, allowing the pain to come forward and intensify.

~Say, **"Orange,"** out loud from your heart. Orange is a warm healing energy that absorbs trapped pain or stress and enables the area to accept a healing. Take a few moments to allow the orange to work. Next, say, **"Release,"** out loud from your heart. Feel the pain leave through your feet, hands, or crown. Repeat the process a few times if needed. For chronic pain, use this technique daily.

Tips for specific areas: For back pain, place a rolled-up hand towel under your back. For arm pain, hold a tennis ball in one hand while pressing on pain area with two fingers. For leg or knee pain, place a tennis ball under one foot while pressing on pain area with two fingers. Firmly grasp shoulders with hands for stress or pain release.

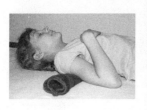   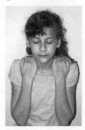

Headache Technique

Key Phrase: "Center-Core-Forward-Lavender-Release"

~Sit or lie back for a few moments and close your eyes. Move your focus from head to heart, placing one hand on the middle of your chest. Focus there and say the key words, **"Center-Core,"** out loud slowly from your heart.

~Place one hand over your forehead (to calm the mental chatter) and the other hand on the base of your skull (your "fight or flight" area).

~Say the key word, **"Forward."** This releases the band of will, allowing the pain to come forward and intensify.

~Say, **"Lavender,"** out loud from your heart. Lavender is a calm healing energy that softens and absorbs trapped pain or stress within the body. Take a few moments to allow the lavender color to work.

~Next say, **"Release,"** out loud from your heart. Feel the pain leave through your crown. Repeat the process a few times as needed.

Quick Version: Lie down, close your eyes and place one hand over your forehead and the other on the base of your skull. Focus at your heart and say, **"Forward,"** out loud from your heart. Soften and absorb the pain by saying, **"Lavender."** Say, **"Release,"** out loud from your heart, allowing the pain to leave.

This exercise relieves headaches, mental fatigue and insomnia.

Balancing Technique

Key Phrase: "Center-Core-Connect-Activate-(Intention)"

~Place one hand on the middle of your chest. Say, **"Center-Core,"** out loud from your heart center. This engages your core structure.

~Place your hands on your lap, palms facing the ceiling. Say, **"Connect,"** from your heart. When you sense an energy connection on your hands, you are ready.

~Choose an aspect of your life that needs attention—attaining a goal, balancing a relationship, releasing a pattern or healing physical, emotional or mental concerns.

~Hold your hands 8 to 10 inches apart facing each other. Select one hand to represent a goal, pattern, issue or concern. The other hand signifies your core. For situations involving relationships, one hand represents the person and the opposite hand represents you.

New Job 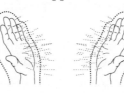 *Your Core*

~Next, assess the situation energetically, by saying, **"Activate."** Sense the energy in front of each hand. Does it feel imbalanced or blocked? Which hand is it? The one representing you? Another person? The situation? Both hands? This provides insight into the situation.

~Create a new structure based on trust. Say the key word, **"Trust."** Clear the pathway energetically by choosing an intention and saying it from your heart. Some examples are, **"Integrate, Balance, Heal, Manifest, Openness, Communication, Transform, Release, Neutralize, Best possible outcome, Empower."** Once the situation is energetically balanced, the change quickly manifests in the physical world.

Healing Hands Technique

This technique provides a quick way to balance and integrate the functions and elements. The thumb and first three fingers signify the four elements and their corresponding functions based on Carl Jung's four psychological types: thinking-air function, intuition-fire function, sensing-earth function and feeling-water function. The little finger signifies the integration of ether and inner core energy used to infuse both elements and functions.

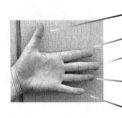
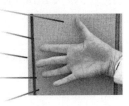

Thinking - Air Function
Intuition - Fire Function
Sensing - Earth Function
Feeling - Water Function
Integration - Ether - Core

~Your two hands respectively represent your conscious and subconscious parts of self. If you are right-handed, this hand represents your conscious self. Your left hand signifies your subconscious self. If you are a left-handed person, the opposite is true.

~Starting with the right hand, place the tip of your thumb between your opposite thumb and index finger, pressing firmly for 15 seconds. As you close your eyes and apply pressure to your thumb, notice the corresponding body response. You may feel a tightness, sensitivity or pain. If so, wiggle the thumb for fifteen seconds to clear and balance this area. Then ground this area by holding the thumb firmly for the same amount of time. Continue until the area feels calm. Repeat the process with the opposite thumb.

~Continue with each finger, paying attention to your body responses. This technique releases trapped pain and stress throughout the body and integrates the elements and functions, infusing them with ether and inner core energy.

These are much needed skills

in a world

that has forgotten its roots...

Reclaim your own

Conclusion

*You have to leave the city of your comfort
and go into the wilderness of your intuition.
What you discover will be wonderful.
What you discover will be yourself.*
—Alan Alda

All of us possess untapped inner instincts and senses just waiting to be discovered. Take the time to explore your distinct qualities and attributes. The reward is the gift of self-discovery.

As you begin your day, align with life's flow and allow your inner core to lead the way. Shift your focus to your heart and experience the undiluted moment, tapping into the magic the day offers. **Life slows down and there is time for reflection as well as productivity.**

During the day, relax the overworked mind, transforming it into a state of mindfulness. Release depressed or repressed emotions to gain emotional intelligence. Return your physical body to its natural state, its instinctual nature. Infuse inner core energy throughout your psyche, initiating the move toward higher consciousness and wisdom.

The survival skills in this book are designed to fit your busy lifestyle. As you become familiar with these skills, feel free to customize and make them your own.

As you deepen your relationship with your intuition, you'll find it expresses and teaches you its unique language in surprising ways. For example, there are times when my *yes* response from my insight changes to a *thumbs up* response. I interpret this as a firm confirmation, that I am asking the right questions and interpreting the answers correctly.

133

When using the Balancing Technique, if I choose an intention that doesn't quite fit, one of my hands will turn away from the other. This is a signal from my insight that there is a better intention that fits the situation more succinctly. The more you practice getting to know your inner instincts, insight and inner core, the more you'll express your true self.

Change is happening more quickly than ever. Adaptability, instinct and insight are the survival skills most needed in this fast-paced world. Learn to integrate and utilize your inner and outer resources. Together, they provide the courage and inner security to not only survive, but thrive.

There is a deep and ancient connection that flows through everything and everyone on this beautiful planet. Although life seems chaotic and uncertain, we are blessed to be alive at this moment in time; our actions should reflect this. Do your part by sinking into the earth, allowing her ancient roots to ground and remind you—that you too are an important and integral part of life.

Glossary

Acupressure: An ancient healing art that uses the fingers to press key points on the skin to stimulate the body's natural healing.

Aura: A luminous radiation that emanates from all living matter; a distinctive atmosphere surrounding a given source.

Awareness: The ability to recognize, understand and transform what is happening around us.

Balance: Even distribution of weight or amount; stability of mind and body.

Chakra: Energy centers within the body, the spinning of which generates an electromagnetic field in and around the body.

Clairaudience: The ability to hear sounds inaudible to the normal ear; being attuned to the spirit world.

Clairsentience: A highly sensitive empathetic ability to experience the world through the function of feeling.

Clairvoyance: The ability to see or perceive the inner and outer world with no constraints of time or space.

Earth energy: A calming energy originating from the core of the earth.

Elements: Four substances (air, fire, earth, water) mentioned in ancient Medieval philosophy.

Empathy: Capacity to identify with a person or object.

Energy: Force, vigor, capacity for activity.

Energy centers: Cones or small speakers located throughout the body that send and receive information.

Etheric level: A net-like layer surrounding the physical body extending out a few inches that acts as a buffer between body and emotions.

Focus: A position where something is placed for clarity of perception.

Functions: Different modes of processing or perceiving.

Grounding: Renew the connection between physical body and earth.

Inner core: Your true self who holds your purpose and potential.

Insight: The power or act of seeing into a situation.

Instinct: Innate pattern of behavior; unconscious skill.

Intention: What one hopes to do or bring about.

Intuition: The ability to obtain direct knowledge without use of rational thought.

Kinesiology: A diagnostic method using manual muscle testing and therapy.

Knowingness: A strong conviction or inner knowing.

Levels: Different locations and functions of the aura.

Mental focus: A mind focus; predominantly using a thought-based or logical approach.

Meridian: An energy channel within the body.

Muscle testing: A non-invasive way of evaluating the body's imbalances and assessing its needs.

Overuse of will: An imbalance of will resorting to rigidity and control.

Pain: The sensation that is felt when you are hurt physically, emotionally, or mentally.

Perception: Act or faculty of perceiving; intuitive recognition of truth.

Personal space: A three-feet area of energy surrounding the body.

Psychometry: The ability to sense and interpret energy emanating from inanimate objects.

Sensing: Stimuli from inside or outside the body that is received and felt through the five senses.

Speaker: An energy center located in or around the body.

Strength: An aptitude for letting go, adapting and flowing with life.

Stress: Pressure that is affecting something or someone due to an external force.

Universal energy: A light, airy energy that comes from the universe.

Whole body awareness: A natural state of being; all parts of self working together.

Will: A driving force within you to accomplish or achieve something.

Insights & Notes

Insights & Notes

About the Author

Gina Giacomini, intuitive, motivational speaker and author, has taught inner awareness courses for twenty years. With a background in education and outdoor adventure, Gina shares her survival skills for today's fast-paced world. Her books include *Bringing Intuition to Work,* published in the U.S. and Germany, and *Intuition: The Key to Divination,* published by Random House UK.

E-mail: gina@stresspainrelease.com
Website: www.stresspainrelease.com

Order Form

Quantity	Item	Amount

Go with the Flow
Stress & Pain Release Guide ($14.95)
_____
Sales tax of 8.25% for California residents
Shipping and Handling (see chart below)
Total:

Amount blanks: _____ for Guide, _____ for sales tax, _____ for shipping, _____ for Total

Quantity discounts available
Shipping and handling

	1st Class	Priority	1 to 4 Books
United States	varies	$4.95	same

Method of Payment

Check or money order enclosed
(make payable to Gina Giacomini in U.S. currency only)

Please photocopy this order form, fill it out and mail it together with your name, address, personal check or money order to:

INNERVISIONS
PUBLICATIONS

P. O. Box 213
Coloma, CA 95613

E-mail: gina@stresspainrelease.com
Website: www.stresspainrelease.com